Understanding
Faith
Formation

Understanding Faith Formation

*Theological, Congregational,
and Global Dimensions*

Mark A. Maddix, Jonathan H. Kim,
and James Riley Estep Jr.

Baker Academic

a division of Baker Publishing Group
Grand Rapids, Michigan

Published by Baker Academic
a division of Baker Publishing Group
PO Box 6287, Grand Rapids, MI 49516-6287
www.bakeracademic.com

Printed in the United States of America

Library of Congress Cataloging-in-Publication Data
Names: Maddix, Mark A., 1965– author. | Kim, Jonathan H., author. | Estep, James Riley, 1963– author.
Title: Understanding faith formation : theological, congregational, and global dimensions / Mark A. Maddix, Jonathan H. Kim, and James Riley Estep, Jr.
Description: Grand Rapids, Michigan : Baker Academic, a division of Baker Publishing Group, 2020. | Includes index.
Identifiers: LCCN 2020018322 | ISBN 9781540960382 (paperback) | ISBN 9781540963451 (casebound)
Subjects: LCSH: Faith development.
Classification: LCC BT771.3 .M34 2020 | DDC 268—dc23
LC record available at https://lccn.loc.gov/2020018322

20 21 22 23 24 25 26   7 6 5 4 3 2 1

In keeping with biblical principles of creation stewardship, Baker Publishing Group advocates the responsible use of our natural resources. As a member of the Green Press Initiative, our company uses recycled paper when possible. The text paper of this book is composed in part of post-consumer waste.

Contents

Introduction

Dimensions of Faith Formation

As you pick up this book, you might be wondering, "Why another book on faith formation? Hasn't enough already been written about this topic?" If you are asking these questions, you are not alone. As authors, we raised the same questions when contemplating writing this book. We acknowledge that significant work has been done in this area, particularly since the rediscovery of ancient spiritual formation practices. The surge of literature on spiritual formation has brought it to the mainstream of the church. We also recognize that James Fowler's *Stages of Faith* was written over four decades ago and has since received significant praise and criticism in the literature. Fowler's influence on the field is unparalleled and has provided significant research in how persons develop faith. Both progressive and conservative scholars have provided ample research building on Fowler's theory to advance the discussion of faith formation.

Yet at the same time, we recognize that religiosity and faith development are in decline in the North American Christian context, particularly when it comes to church attendance and participation in Christian practices. The growth of the nones, those who have no religious faith, is affecting how faith is being expressed in our context. Religious apathy reflected as Moral Therapeutic Deism and a lack of biblical literacy have resulted in a recipe for frustration and concern among Christian faith communities. The church has good reason to be concerned about the next generation's faith formation.

In light of these concerns, we believe that a book on faith formation is needed to address the theological, congregational, and global dimensions of faith formation. As authors, we are well versed in the literature of faith formation and believe that a book on faith formation can help educators, pastors, and church leaders understand and practice their faith more deeply. We also believe that there is a great desire among Christians to embrace new avenues of spiritual growth and development, particularly in the midst of a culturally diverse world.

Book Content and Design

This book, titled *Understanding Faith Formation: Theological, Congregational, and Global Dimensions*, is an attempt to develop an integrated and holistic approach to faith formation that has a strong biblical and theological core. We use the term *dimensions*, a mathematical term that means to give dimensions and properties to an area. Faith requires certain properties necessary for its formation. Our dimensions of theological, congregational, and global are three interwoven dimensions that work together to provide Christians with a framework for faith formation. All dimensions are necessary, and when one aspect is neglected, it hinders a person's growth. Figure 1 provides an illustration of how these three dimensions work together.

The book is divided into three parts. Part 1 focuses on the *theological dimensions of faith formation*. Chapter 1 defines and traces the meaning of faith through the Old and New Testaments. Chapter 2 reviews faith formation from the perspectives of the major movements in Christian tradition.

Figure 1
Dimensions of Faith Formation

Chapter 3 summarizes James Fowler's theory of faith development and the development of an evangelical view of faith formation. Chapter 4 provides a critique and the limitations of Fowler's theory based on content, structuralism, gender, and diversity.

Part 2 focuses on the *congregational dimensions of faith formation*. Chapter 5 explores the cultural challenges to faith formation, including biblical illiteracy, Moral Therapeutic Deism, and the rise of the nones. Chapter 6 illustrates the role that congregations play in forming faith through their rituals and practices. Particular attention is given to faith formation through worship, fellowship, preaching, mission and service, and justice. Chapter 7 focuses on viewing Scripture less as *information* and more as *formation*. The thesis is that Scripture was given to the church as a means to form persons into Christlikeness.

Part 3 focuses on the *global dimensions of faith formation*. Chapter 8 illustrates the powerful transformation that takes place as people engage in cross-cultural mission trips. As people engage in cross-cultural experiences, they experience disequilibration that results in learning and growth. Chapter 9 focuses on the multiethnic and multicultural dimensions of the diversity of the kingdom of God, noting that cultural context is critical in understanding faith formation. Chapter 10 provides an understanding of faith formation outside North America by focusing on faith formation in global contexts.

Discussion questions and suggestions for further reading are provided at the end of each chapter so that the book can be used in an academic classroom, Sunday school class, or small group. The book is designed to help people engage in conversation about matters of faith and how faith is formed in a person's life. We hope this isn't just an academic exercise but a resource to help people grow in their Christian faith.

Case Study

One way to illustrate the theological, congregational, and global dimensions of faith formation is through a case study. Janet is a white female who is in her forties and has been a person of faith for many years. As Janet studies the Bible with other Christians and learns more about a biblical understanding of faith as expressed in Scripture, her faith is being developed through the *theological dimension*. As she participates in the regular rhythms and patterns of worship as an active member of her local church, her faith is being developed through the *congregational dimension*. And because Janet is part of a congregation that consists of people from a variety of ethnic contexts, her faith is being developed through the *global dimension*. How she grows in her faith may be very different from how believers from different ethnic contexts grow in their faith, and she will need to own her own biases and limitations in order to understand more fully the diversity of the kingdom of God.

Faithful Reading

As you read this book, whether for assigned reading in class or as part of a discussion group or Bible study, we encourage you to enter into the narrative by placing yourself in the dimensions of faith formation. In other words, we would like you to consider where you are in your faith formation and what practices you need to develop to continue to nurture your faith. We also ask that you consider your own context, whether you are in a monolithic context, with people who look and act like you, or a multiethnic context, with people who are very different from you. Faith is always expressed and lived out in a particular context that requires you to reexamine some of your presuppositions about your faith and to recognize that people from other cultures may mature in their faith in different ways.

We wrote this book because of our love for people, for the growth of the church, and for the kingdom of God. It is our prayer that the reading and the discussion of this book will increase your faith and Christian practice and ultimately help you grow in your relationship with God.

Part 1

Theological Dimensions of Faith Formation

1

Faith Formation in the Bible

One of the authors remembers going shopping with his daughter. After wandering through countless similar stores for a couple of hours, he finally broke down and asked, "Have you found anything?" She replied, "I don't know what I'm looking for, but I'll know it when I see it." Faith is like that. *Faith* is a word often used but rarely defined. We recognize it when we encounter it but find it difficult to explain. In fact, most would be hard-pressed to express a coherent or encompassing description of faith. When asked about faith or faith formation, believers often react with a list of synonyms, like *trust, fidelity, growth,* or *maturing,* or they quickly quote Hebrews 11:1: "Now faith is the assurance of things hoped for, the conviction of things not seen." However, as a concept, faith usually remains more ill-defined and elusive than often realized.

For example, faith is what we believe—that is, *the faith* (Jude 3, 20)—but we are also saved by grace *through faith* (Eph. 2:8), walk *by faith* (2 Cor. 5:7), and live *by faith* (Rom. 1:17, citing Hab. 2:4). In fact, the author of Hebrews asserts, "And without faith it is impossible to please him, for whoever would draw near to God must believe that he exists and that he rewards those who seek him" (11:6). Faith is the identifying mark of a Christ follower (Acts 10:45; 1 Thess. 1:6–7), but how is faith formed? How do believers grow in Christ?

To ascertain the biblical concept of faith formation, one has to sift through the vocabulary of Scripture as well as through all the passages on faith, belief, and faithfulness so as to filter out irrelevant passages and concentrate on those passages that provide insight into the process of faith formation in the life of the believer. It is not enough to do a lexical or grammatical study of faith in the Old and New Testaments; we also have to study their contexts so as to determine the processes, contributing factors, and even deterrents to faith formation.

Likewise, the theological traditions that comprise the heritage of Christianity often reflect the church's wrestling with questions surrounding the nature of faith and its formation, and hence the biblical and the theological must be engaged in concert with each other. This chapter draws a portrait of faith and its formation as it occurs in the Old and New Testaments, providing a picture or snapshot of the subject, while chapter 2 presents a moving picture, a film, of how the church's theological traditions have addressed central issues in understanding the germination of faith and how it forms.

Faith in the Old Testament

When one reads the Hebrew Bible, perhaps one of the first observations that can be made regarding faith is that there is an apparent *absence* of faith as one may recognize it. While the word most often translated "believe" or "faith" (*ēmūnah*) occurs ninety-six times throughout the Old Testament, it most frequently is *not* used to describe the Hebrews' relationship with God. Rather, it is most often about human relations. The word *ēmūn* has a much broader meaning and occurs in a wide variety of contexts, requiring more contextualized translations. It basically means "to be firm, endure, be faithful, be true, stand fast, trust, have belief, believe," with similar parallels in Aramaic, Arabic, and Syriac. For this reason, the translations of the Old Testament rarely translate it as religious faith. For example, the King James Version translates *ēmūn* as "faith" only twice, and the Revised Standard Version translates it this way only eighteen times. This is because the term *ēmūn* is rarely placed in a religious or personal context, more often being used in a legal context regarding covenants—that is, breaking or keeping faith between two people or nations (see Lev. 5:15; Deut. 32:51; Judg. 9:15–21).[1]

But if faith is not the basic description of a relationship with God in the Old Testament, what is? The Old Testament describes humans' relationship with God as one of fear and trust.[2] Joseph P. Healey also correctly observes that "faith is described rather than defined in the Hebrew Bible. The description tends to be used in two ways, one where the relationship of Israel to Yahweh is described and the other where the relationship of certain key figures to Yahweh is described [e.g., Abraham, David, and the prophets]. The common characteristic of the two are their unswerving loyalty to Yahweh even in the face of what appear to be insurmountable obstacles, and second is the purely gratuitous character of their chosenness."[3]

Faith as a basis for relating to God is not readily found in the Hebrew Bible, but several instances do stand out in which faith is indeed a response to God and hence does occur in a more religious context than is typical. For example:

- "And he *believed* the LORD, and he counted it to him as righteousness." (Gen. 15:6)
- "And Israel saw the great power that the LORD used against the Egyptians, so the people feared the LORD, and they *believed* in the LORD and in his servant Moses." (Exod. 14:31)
- "And he said, 'I will hide my face from them; I will see what their end will be, for they are a perverse generation, children in whom is no *faithfulness.*'" (Deut. 32:20)
- "Behold, his soul is puffed up; it is not upright within him, but the righteous shall live by his *faith.*" (Hab. 2:4)

However, such passages are relatively few, especially in comparison to the New Testament's treatment of faith. While *ēmūn* and its derivatives occur throughout the Old Testament, "with at least ten distinct categories in which the noun is used in Scripture," eventually it "moves almost entirely to the use of the word in connection with God or those related to God" and primarily to describe God himself.[4] The use of *ēmūn* applied only to God is further borne out by the fact that when God is the subject or the object of the verb, the Septuagint (LXX) translates it with *pisteuō* ("believe") exclusively, with the exception of Proverbs 26:25.

In short, a study of faith in the Old Testament reveals more about God than it does about the faith of the Hebrew people. Therefore, while the Old Testament does serve as a background for better understanding Christian faith, to understand the nature, function, and formation of faith, we have to rely on the New Testament.

Faith in the New Testament

Faith is a more prominent topic and frequently occurring theme in the New Testament than in the Old Testament. Both the noun *pistis*, translated "faith," and its verb form *pisteuō*, translated "believe," are more prevalent, occurring over 240 times, with the adjective *pistos* ("faithful") occurring 67 times. This word occurs in a variety of contexts, with each New Testament author nuancing its use; for example, the noun *faith* never occurs in John's Gospel, whereas it is frequently used in Paul's writings. However, its use as the principle means of describing our response to and relationship with God is indeed consistent throughout the New Testament, and this use is unique in the ancient world. Dieter Lührmann notes that this notion of faith, the religious idea of faith, is almost exclusively a Christian concept, not even occurring in Hellenistic texts.[5] Hence, while the word *faith* is nuanced differently throughout the New Testament,[6] the use of *faith* in a religious context is distinctive to early Christian beliefs.

Faith conveys the idea of being persuaded and living a life consistent with a newfound truth—that is, the gospel.[7] The New Testament word for *faith*, unlike its Old Testament antecedent, especially brings out "the main elements in faith in its relation to the invisible God, as distinct from faith in man."[8] Most times in the New Testament, faith is used in the context of trust and confidence in God.[9] It is the process of coming to faith, perhaps the verb form, *pisteuō*, that occurs ninety-eight times in the Gospel of John alone. Given his purpose in writing, this is understandable: "Now Jesus did many other signs in the presence of the disciples, which are not written in this book; but these are written so that you may *believe* that Jesus is the Christ, the Son of God, and that by *believing* you may have life in his name" (John 20:30–31).[10]

Toward a Biblical Model of Faith

Based on the concept of faith in the New Testament and in the Old, a composite picture of faith, a snapshot, can be formed. A common idea of faith used throughout the centuries has been a threefold faith centered on Christ through the mind, the will, and action. While faith is indeed a gift of God (John 3:3; 1 Cor. 2:14; 2 Cor. 4:4–6; Eph. 2:1–4) and not merely a human attainment, as will be discussed in the next chapter, the biblical witness shows that faith has these three dimensions. While numerous sources affirm this view, Gregg R. Allison provides a recent and thorough treatment of faith in the Bible. He describes our "holistic response" to God in faith as a matter of "rightly affirming the truth (*orthodoxy*), rightly feeling the truth (*orthopatheia*), and rightly practicing the faith (*orthopraxis*)."[11] Figure 1.1 depicts his idea.

Along the same line, Healey notes that in the Old Testament, faith is connected to remembrance (cognition), overcoming fear (affection), and doing (volition).[12] In the New Testament, when Paul writes to Timothy in 2 Timothy 3:14–17, he reminds him that Scripture's formative influence includes the mind ("acquainted with the sacred writings, which are able to make you wise for

Figure 1.1

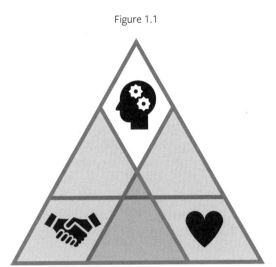

salvation," v. 15); will ("all Scripture is breathed out by God," v. 16); and life transformation ("profitable for teaching, for reproof, for correction, and for training in righteousness," v. 16), so "that the man of God may be complete, equipped for every good work" (v. 17).

Here is a breakdown of Paul's threefold model of faith in Christ.

"Believe that . . .": faith as cognition. Sometimes the noun *pistis* denotes the content or object of our faith, what we believe (Rom. 1:5; Gal. 1:23; 1 Tim. 4:1, 6; James 2:14–16; Jude 3). Beyond the notion of faith being a noun—that is, the faith—it is in part also what we believe and a means of knowing. We know and wrestle with truth by reasoning, but having faith is also part of our way of knowing. "For we walk by faith, not by sight" (2 Cor. 5:7). Similarly, Paul explains the cognitive dimension of faith in 2 Thessalonians 2:11–12, writing, "Therefore God sends them a strong delusion, so that they may believe what is false, in order that all may be condemned who did not believe the truth but had pleasure in unrighteousness." The relationship between faith and reason will be explored more in the following chapter, but for now, note that Scripture indeed includes cognition as a vital aspect of faith. The object or subject of faith is crucial since faith is not separate from what we place our faith in.

"Believe in . . .": faith as trust. Romans 1:18–25 explains that humanity has the ability to intellectually affirm the existence and power of God, but that is only one kind of faith. Biblical faith is not the mere affirmation or acknowledgment of a propositional truth but placing trust, certainty, in it. As previously noted, in the Old Testament, trust is the concept that often parallels

faith in the New Testament, and the sentiments of Psalm 31:14 echo this: "But I trust in you, O LORD; I say, 'You are my God.'" Faith builds a relationship with God by placing trust in him. This is why John could pen, "But to all who did receive him, *who believed in his name*, he gave the right to become children of God" (John 1:12). This is the difference between knowing about God and knowing God.

"Faithful": faith resulting in service. While faith is not equivalent to works, a life of faith should manifest itself in works of service. Paul states in Ephesians 2:10, "For we are his workmanship, created in Christ Jesus for good works, which God prepared beforehand, that we should walk in them." And James 2:22 says, "You see that faith was active along with his works, and faith was completed by his works." Genuine faith is reflected in a genuine change of life, manifested by fruitfulness, service, and good works—not for salvation but because of it.

Biblical Insights into Faith Formation

It is important to differentiate between faith formation and faith development. This is not just a matter of semantics; the distinction between formative processes and developmental processes is significant. Oftentimes the term *faith development* is associated with theories of a more psychological nature, such as those of James W. Fowler and Fritz Oser,[13] which emphasize the human phenomenon of faith. *Faith formation* leans less on psychology and human development and more on what James E. Loder described as the transforming moment, not an innate, purely human experience but a divine encounter.[14]

Scripture contains numerous metaphors for faith formation, such as maturing (e.g., 1 Cor. 2:6; Eph. 4:12–13; Phil. 3:15; Col. 4:12; Heb. 5:14; James 1:4), bearing fruit (Isa. 5; John 15:1–16; Gal. 5:19–23), and the process of growth (1 Cor. 3:6–7; 2 Cor. 10:15; Eph. 2:21; 4:14–16; Col. 1:10; 3:10; 2 Pet. 3:18). However, as valuable as a metaphor may be, it rarely conveys specific detail about the actual process of faith formation or what contributes to it. Several passages of Scripture provide more specific insight into faith formation in the believer, giving direction and substance to the process, as will be discussed later in this chapter.

Paul admonishes the Corinthians, "We do not boast beyond limit in the labors of others. But our hope is that *as your faith increases*, our area of influence among you may be greatly enlarged" (2 Cor. 10:15). Faith is often not 100 percent but a balance between believing and wrestling with disbelief. The transparency of the father who asked Jesus to heal his child displays this:

"Immediately the father of the child cried out and said, '*I believe; help my unbelief!*'" (Mark 9:24). Faith may have its starting point, but it is also meant to increase, gaining ascendency over our unbelief so as to characterize our lives. This is echoed by Paul when he writes about those who are "weak in faith" as opposed to others (Rom. 14:1–4).

A Vocabulary Lesson

Based on the use of terms related to faith in the Scriptures, a relationship between these terms begins to emerge when focusing on the subject of faith formation. Generally speaking, the faith (*pistis*) is believed (*pisteuō*) and produces belief/faith (*pistis*) that grows into the characteristic in life recognized as faithfulness (*pistos*).

The faith (pistis). The faith, referring to the content of what we believe, is highlighted in Jude 3: "Beloved, although I was very eager to write to you about our common salvation, I found it necessary to write appealing to you to *contend for the faith* that was once for all delivered to the saints." Christian faith does not exist in isolation, nor can it be self-vindicating. Faith needs a core, a center, something beyond ourselves on which it is positioned. In this regard, the center of faith is Christ, the gospel, or God's Word or truth.

Believe (pisteuō). The verb *believe* requires an object and usually a preposition, for example, believes *that, in, into,* or *on,* denoting that the faith is not self-based but based on something else—that is, the faith.[15] J. I. Packer acknowledges this: "The complexity of this idea [that faith requires an object] is reflected in the various constructions used with the verb [*pisteuō*]."[16] *Believe that, pisteuein hoti* (Heb. 11:6; cf. John 2:22; 2 Thess. 2:12) emphasizes what is believed. *Believe in, pisteuein ev* (Mark 1:15; John 3:15; Eph. 1:13), believe *into, pisteuein eis* (John 1:12; Acts 10:43; 1 John 5:10), and occasionally *believe on, pisteuein epi* (1 Tim. 1:16), denote confidence in the object of faith—that is, Jesus. Belief *unto, pisteuein eis* (John 2:11; 3:16; 4:39; 14:1; Gal. 2:16; Phil. 1:29), signifies an action toward the object of faith, most typically Christ.[17] Prepositions matter!

Belief/faith (pistis). Hebrews 11:1–3 says, "Now *faith* is the assurance of things hoped for, the conviction of things not seen. For *by it* [faith] the people of old received their commendation. *By faith* . . ." Faith is now something we possess, derived from the source of faith through the process of believing. Believing leaves a deposit of belief. Belief *that* is an affirming faith; for example, "I believe that" something is true. Belief *in, into,* or *on* connotes more than an affirming faith. It is a personal trust, commitment, or conviction that over time will begin to influence one's identity and character.[18] The most common construction found in the New Testament (*pisteuein eis* or *epi* used with the accusative), which is virtually absent in the LXX and does not occur in classical Greek literature, expresses the process of moving out in trust, embracing the object of faith, and proceeding in confidence from it.[19] Believing leads to belief.

Faithfulness (pistos). This is a descriptive quality of a consistent, dependable relationship—for example, between two people or, more frequently in the New Testament, between God and a person or even a congregation. This is the case with Timothy (1 Cor. 4:17), Onesimus (Col. 4:9), Epaphras (Col. 1:7), Tychicus (Eph. 6:21; Col. 4:7), and the churches in Ephesus and Colossae (Eph. 1:1; Col. 1:2). This is a quality attributed to both God and humans, with morality being a communicable attribute. God's absolute faithfulness and humanity's relative faithfulness to him are noteworthy, particularly in the Old Testament but in the New Testament as well.[20] Faithfulness is a quality of a mature, consistent, and pervasive faith in the life of the believer, the result of believing the faith over a long period, or as Eugene H. Peterson described the Christian life, "a long obedience in the same direction."[21]

Add to Your Faith

Scripture describes faith as a gift, something we must rely on another to give to us. This has been echoed by the theologians of the church. But at the same time, the New Testament doesn't treat faith as something instantaneous or as something that is immediately attained in its fullness. Rather, several passages insist that faith requires our attention if it is going to increase and reach maturity. Peter writes:

> To those who have *obtained a faith of equal standing with ours* by the righteousness of our God and Savior Jesus Christ. . . . His divine power has granted to us all things that pertain to life and godliness, through the knowledge of him who called us to his own glory and excellence, by which he has granted to us his precious and very great promises, so that through them you may become partakers of the divine nature, having escaped from the corruption that is in the world because of sinful desire. For this very reason, *make every effort to supplement your faith* with virtue, and virtue with knowledge, and knowledge with self-control, and self-control with steadfastness, and steadfastness with godliness, and godliness with brotherly affection, and brotherly affection with love. *For if these qualities are yours and are increasing, they keep you from being ineffective or unfruitful in the knowledge of our Lord Jesus Christ.* For whoever lacks these qualities is so nearsighted that he is blind, having forgotten that he was cleansed from his former sins. Therefore, brothers, be all the more diligent

to confirm your calling and election, *for if you practice these qualities you will never fall.* For in this way there will be richly provided for you an entrance into the eternal kingdom of our Lord and Savior Jesus Christ. (2 Pet. 1:1, 3–11)

Obviously, even if faith is a gift of God, we are instructed to care for it by adding to it qualities to insulate it and ensure its continued presence in our lives. Similarly, in perhaps one of the most controversial passages in the New Testament, James challenges the Christians in the diaspora to make their faith more tangible.

But someone will say, "You have faith and I have works." Show me your faith apart from your works, and I will show you my faith by my works. You believe that God is one; you do well. Even the demons believe—and shudder! Do you want to be shown, you foolish person, that faith apart from works is useless? Was not Abraham our father justified by works when he offered up his son Isaac on the altar? You see that faith was active along with his works, and faith was completed by his works; and the Scripture was fulfilled that says, "Abraham believed God, and it was counted to him as righteousness"—and he was called a friend of God. You see that a person is justified by works and not by faith alone. And in the same way was not also Rahab the prostitute justified by works when she received the messengers and sent them out by another way? For as the body apart from the spirit is dead, so also faith apart from works is dead. (James 2:18–26)

 This passage readily demonstrates that a faith that does not increase, does not grow, or remains intellectualized or merely inert in one's life is not the kind of faith James maintains a believer should have or needs to have for a robust Christian walk.

faith = must grow

What about *Faith* and *Spirituality*?

It is common, and in fact too common, in contemporary vernacular for the terms *faith* and *spirituality* to be used synonymously, almost interchangeably. While it is not wrong to create a term to describe a biblical concept, confusing it with the biblical concept can lead to distortion.

The term *spirituality* is not found in Scripture. This is not a matter of translation preference or translation bias; rather, the original languages of the Bible simply do not have a word for it. The term was introduced in the seventeenth century by French Catholic theologians and eventually made its way into Protestant theology in the nineteenth century and later into evangelical discourse.[22] The words S/*spirit* (*pneuma*) and *spiritual* (*pneumatikos*) are used in the New Testament on numerous occasions, but they are distinct from its use of *faith*.

What else distinguishes these terms?

First, *spiritual* is exclusively a New Testament term. While the work of the Holy Spirit is present in both Testaments, his work is far more pronounced in the New Testament.[23] It should be no surprise, then, that a survey of an English concordance demonstrates that the word *spiritual* is absent from the Old Testament. Whereas the Greek πνεῦμα (*pneuma*), *Spirit*, in the New Testament finds its equivalent with the Hebrew רוּחַ (*ruach*) in the Old Testament, no equivalent exists that matches the Greek πνευματικός (*pneumatikos*), *spiritual*, in the Hebrew Bible. Again, this is not a matter of translation preference or bias; there is simply no word in ancient Hebrew for *spiritual*.

Second, while both *spiritual* and *faithful* are adjectives, requiring an object to modify, their application is distinctively different. The term *spiritual* is used in the New Testament in regard to a variety of animate and inanimate objects, denoting a state of being or quality of being celestial, heavenly, not originating from or limited by this world, or purposed for something other than the temporal. Table 1.1 contains a list of things described as spiritual in the Bible.

Table 1.1
Spiritual Things in the Bible

gifts (Rom. 1:11; 1 Cor. 1:7; 12:1; 14:1, 12, 37)	seed (1 Cor. 9:11)
law (Rom. 7:14)	nourishment (1 Cor. 10:3; 1 Pet. 2:2)
worship (Rom. 12:1; 1 Pet. 2:5)	rock (1 Cor. 10:4)
fervor (Rom. 12:11)	resurrected/heavenly body (1 Cor. 15:44)
blessing (Rom. 15:27; Eph. 1:3)	opposite of natural (1 Cor. 15:46)
truth (1 Cor. 2:13)	songs (Eph. 5:19; Col. 3:16)
discernment (1 Cor. 2:14)	anti-Christian forces (Eph. 6:12)
words (1 Cor. 2:13)	wisdom (Col. 1:9)
man (1 Cor. 2:15)	house/dwelling (1 Pet. 2:5)
status (1 Cor. 3:1; Gal. 6:1)	

Faithful, however, is applied to a narrower list of subjects, most typically people and their ministry or God's/Christ's faithfulness toward us. It is not used in regard to an inanimate object, with the possible exception of "faithful saying" (*pistos ho logos*) in the Pastoral Epistles (1 Tim. 1:15; 4:9; 2 Tim. 2:11–13; Titus 3:8). While the two terms may be related, they are not interchangeable, and the concept of spiritual seems to be more broadly encompassing than that of faithful.

Finally, spirituality and faith are not mutually exclusive but complementary, meaning we must explain their relationship. While spirituality and faith are not synonymous, they do not negate each other's significance in the life of the believer. Spirituality seems to have a more experiential dimension, with a limited connection to cognition or rationale, a connection that is often relegated more to faith.[24]

Conclusion

There is more to defining faith in the Scriptures than what might be first realized. The Old and New Testaments provide distinct portraits of faith—not contradictory but not identical either. Likewise, the vocabulary used to give faith dimension and depth enlightens the study of its meaning, including its distinction from the related, but not identical, concept of spirituality. Faith seems to be both precise in its core but far reaching in its implications for the believer.

Discussion Questions

- In regard to the three dimensions of biblical faith (mind, will, action), which one has primacy in your life?
- Can you identify some things that would increase your faith or some next steps that would aid in your spiritual growth (see 2 Pet. 1:1, 3–11)?
- How would you describe the relationship between faith and spirituality? What factors influence your response?

Further Reading

Estep, James Riley, Jr., Gregg R. Allison, and Michael J. Anthony, eds. A Theology for Christian Education. Nashville: B&H Academic, 2008.

Leclerc, Diane, and Mark A. Maddix. Spiritual Formation: A Wesleyan Paradigm. Kansas City, MO: Beacon Hill, 2011.

Loder, James E. Transforming Moment. Colorado Springs: Helmers & Howard, 1989.

2

Faith Formation in the Christian Tradition

ngaging the subject of faith formation from a theological perspective is rather daunting. Where does one even begin, and how does one proceed from there? Biblical, historical, systematic, canonical, denominational . . . what kind of theology does one employ to address the question of faith formation that is Christian? When studying faith and its formation, it becomes readily apparent that the traditions that comprise the landscape of Christian theology provide responses to the basic questions regarding faith formation. Many of them arose out of the necessity to address the need for faith formation in their contemporary contexts.

This chapter engages faith formation by raising the seminal questions about faith and its formation and then provides a theologically informed response based on Scripture and the Christian traditions most relevant to the questions. Here the subject of faith formation is addressed not as a psychological construct or a wholly human phenomenon but as a theologically defined reality. No single theological tradition of the church can be expected to explain faith formation, and therefore this chapter covers a broad spectrum of Christian traditions, past and present.

How Does Faith Begin? Gifted or Gained?

"A journey of a thousand miles begins with a single step," says the famous Chinese proverb. Everything has a beginning, a starting point—even faith.

Perhaps one of the most fundamental questions in regard to faith formation is, How does faith begin? Is it a gift of God, something we gain for ourselves, or something in between? When the evangelist says, "All you have to do is believe!" this confuses the matter. Is faith something *we* do? Likewise, is it something we *do*, couching it in terms of a meritorious work? Paul reminds us that "not all have faith. But the Lord is faithful" (2 Thess. 3:2–3). Just how does one come to faith?

Scripture affirms that faith is a gift (Rom. 12:3; Eph. 2:4–8; Phil. 1:29). Paul further explains, "For by grace you have been saved through faith. And this is not your own doing; it is the gift of God, not a result of works, so that no one may boast" (Eph. 2:8–9).

Why must faith be a gift? Because without God's assistance, we are dead and not capable of appropriating faith on our own (John 3:3; 1 Cor. 2:14; 2 Cor. 4:4; Eph. 2:1–3; 4:18). As a gift, faith requires the work of the Holy Spirit as the catalytic agent in bringing someone to faith, the beginning of faith formation: "And when he comes, he will convict the world concerning sin and righteousness and judgment: concerning sin, because they do not believe in me" (John 16:8–9). Left to our own devices, we would not come to faith at all. Faith is the result of God's Word (John 5:47; Acts 4:4). "But then will they call on him in whom they have not believed? And how are they to believe in him of whom they have never heard? . . . So faith comes from hearing, and hearing through the word of Christ" (Rom. 10:14, 17). Hence, while we are broken, incapable of discerning the things of God, "dead in our transgressions and sins" (Eph. 2:1), God enables us to come to faith in Christ.

However, there is also a human dimension to faith formation. For example, Peter addresses his second letter "to those who have obtained a faith of equal standing with ours by the righteousness of our God and Savior Jesus Christ," but then he instructs them, "For this very reason, make every effort to *supplement your faith*" (2 Pet. 1:1, 5). The gift is not a supernatural zapping of faith, an instantaneous maturity. One could say that Paul speaks of a saving faith and Peter of a maturing one. In regard to faith formation, both are crucial to understand.

Scripture affirms that on our own, in our broken and darkened state, we could not come to faith without the prompting of God through the Holy Spirit. But if one maintains that faith is wholly divine, a gift that requires no human response, their view is incorrect. At the same time, if one believes that we come to faith on our own, under our own conviction, without any divine assistance, their view is also incorrect. Faith is initiated by God and accepted by us. But how has this been expressed throughout the history of the church?

The Roman Catholic Tradition

The Roman Catholic Church described faith as the leading theological virtue, followed by hope and charity/love (see 1 Cor. 13:13). Whereas cardinal virtues (prudence, temperance, justice, and fortitude) can be practiced by anyone, theological virtues (faith, hope, and love) are gifts granted by the grace of God. "Theological virtues differ from the cardinal virtues because they are not attained by human power but come from God. [They are] conferred by God . . . beyond natural man's ability."[1] Because of our broken nature, faith cannot be *initiated* by humans. One can strive to attain faith, but without divine action, it will never happen. In addition, the Catholic idea of faith as a theological virtue makes the object of one's faith significant.[2] "The disposition of faith is therefore a gift from God by which we are able to act in such a way as to attain God as our goal. As a disposition of the mind, the act toward which faith inclines us is an intellectual one, in which we grasp God as the first truth."[3]

The Reformed and Later Traditions

The Reformation of the sixteenth century stressed faith as a gift of God so as to counter the theological emphasis on works prevalent in the Roman Catholic Church of the time.[4] According to Luther, faith goes beyond knowledge to the heart: "Faith is the yes of the heart, a conviction on which one stakes one's life. On what does faith rest? On Christ."[5] Luther further explains, "It is the peculiar nature of faith to deal with, and to believe, that which is as yet not present. For what is present need not be believed; one feels and sees it. . . . Such a faith cannot fail; for it is based on the Word of God, which is almighty and promises us that if we seek first the kingdom of God and then continue to work, all these things shall be added unto him" (citing Matt. 6:33).[6] Calvin more directly states, "Faith, then, brings a man empty to God, that he may be filled with the blessings of Christ. And so he adds, not of yourselves; that claiming nothing for themselves, they may acknowledge God alone as the author of their salvation."[7] However, as the Reformed tradition moved away from the prevailing Roman Catholic tradition, Jacob Arminius seemed to reappropriate *part* of the Roman Catholic position. The Reformed tradition of Luther and Calvin affirms faith principally as a gift of God and only secondarily as humanity's active dependence on God,[8] and Arminius agrees that the intellectual notion of faith saves.[9]

The balancing act between the divine and the human nature of faith continued into the next generation. John Wesley, an advocate of a more Arminian approach to faith and faith formation, proclaiming that free grace and redemption are available to all, felt compelled to distance himself from his colleague George Whitefield, who gravitated toward the Reformed ideas of election and predestination, with their implications for understanding the beginnings of faith.[10] Wesley's view was that faith is a gift of God, but growth in Christlikeness requires human cooperation through participation in the "means of grace" (practices that help believers experience but not earn God's grace). In other words, faith formation includes a dynamic synergism or cooperation between God and humans. However, Wesley and Whitefield managed to find common grounds of agreement to forge the Methodist movement in eighteenth-century England, with an emphasis on faith formation.[11]

The Modern Church

The nineteenth and twentieth centuries brought new theological traditions, such as classical liberalism, neo-orthodoxy, and psychologizing Christianity. As a result, the pendulum swung away from the notion that faith is a divine gift and toward the human dimension of faith, making it something gained or attained rather than given. "The views of Schleiermacher and Ritschl characterize a great deal of modern liberal theology. Faith, in this theology, is not a heaven-wrought experience, but a human achievement; not the mere receiving of a gift, but a meritorious action."[12] J. I. Packer similarly observes that "liberalism psychologized faith, reducing it to a contented harmony with the Infinite through Christ (Schleiermacher), or fixed resolve to follow Christ's teaching (Ritschl), or both together. Liberal influence appears in the now widespread supposition that 'faith,' understood as optimistic confidence in the universe's friendliness, divorced from any specific creedal tenets, is a distinctively 'spiritual' state of mind."[13] Rudolph Bultmann was seen as anthropomorphizing faith, embedding it strictly in humanity and making it a purely human phenomenon, though some would debate this.[14] In the latter half of the twentieth century, in the face of the Death of God movement, Reinhold Niebuhr understood faith as primarily a sense of identity, providing meaning to human existence and remaining relevant despite modern advances in science.[15]

A Summary of Christian Traditions

Without oversimplifying the matter, the views of Christian traditions could be summarized as making a distinction between faith development and faith formation. Those who see faith in a more human light, even those who approach it as a psychological phenomenon—for example, James W. Fowler in his *Stages of Faith*—tend to use the vocabulary of developmentalism. Those who see faith through the Roman Catholic and Reformation traditions, more religious contexts, tend to emphasize faith as a gift of God. Therefore, a spectrum of faith ranges from gift of God to gained by human ascent (see fig. 2.1).

Figure 2.1

Faith as Gift	Faith as Gained
(*Divine*)	(*Human*)

How Does Reason Relate to Faith?

Unlike many religions that base their truth on an experiential event or subjective leanings, Christianity has historically understood that an individual's faith exists in concert with their intellect. In other words, faith has a cognitive element—*notitia*, as the early church described it. Faith requires right belief about God, even if incomplete (Matt. 9:2, 22, 29; 15:28; Luke 7:50; Acts 19:1–7), meaning that *content* is important to the Christian faith. The content itself must be rational, reasonable, for it to be grasped intellectually. This is the rationale for the place of Scripture—that it allows believers to know, affirm, and obey the truth (Gal. 1:8–9; 2 Thess. 2:13; Titus 1:1; 1 Pet. 1:22). In this regard, Scripture is more than informative for our faith; it is also transformative.[16] The Scriptures were given for "our instruction" (Rom. 15:4), to transform us, and to form our faith.[17]

Christopher Ben Simpson writes, "There is a community between faith and reason—faith has to do with that which is beyond reason, and yet, it is related and in a harmonious relation to reason. Faith entails both certainty and uncertainty. God is knowable to us, but ultimately unknowable. God is transcendent, but also immanent at the same time."[18] Faith and reason, or faith and intellect, are not diametrically opposed: "Rather, faith and reason *both* are we, ourselves living in openness and following the desire to know what is true and love what is good."[19] This relationship between the divine gift of faith and the human faculty of intellect has been a topic of discourse throughout the history of the church. However, the early apologists and those seeking to integrate Greco-Roman philosophy and Christian faith were the first to provide a legacy of faith and reason in the church.

The Patristics Tradition

One reason for the rise of an intellectualized faith in the early church was the threat of Gnosticism. In opposition to it, the church needed to affirm the *regula fidei*, "rule of faith," the ultimate authority or standard in religious belief. "In the debate with Gnosticism, faith was dealt with primarily as the inner determination of faith, which is part of a whole complex of relationships with God, the world, and the human being."[20] As the church sought to repel the Gnostic heresy, the threefold model of faith began to favor the cognitive, intellectual dimension. "The prevalent idea seems to be that of a merely intellectual assent to the truth, but in some cases, it apparently includes the idea of self-surrender," which degraded into Stoic moralism, following the gospel as a *nova lex* ("new law").[21]

The Alexandrian tradition sought to integrate the intellectual pursuits of Christians with those of the Greco-Roman world: faith in relation to philosophy. Essentially, how does faith fit into epistemology? If a suitable response could be offered, it would balance faith and knowledge without surrendering either. Clement and his successor, Origen, viewed *pistis* ("faith") as no match for *gnosis* ("knowledge") if they remained separate. Faith must be a step toward knowledge. "Clement thus characterized Christian experience as one of threefold conversion. First comes the turning from paganism to faith. The turning from faith to knowledge follows. Yet Clement avoids intellectualized abstraction, for from knowledge there should then be the final turning to love, in which is established 'a mutual friendship between the knower and the known.'"[22] However, over the first few centuries of the church, essentially the biblical portrait of an integrated faith involving mind, will, and action was slowly disintegrated, with intellect rising above the others. Later, Augustine explains further:

> The Christian, therefore, can separate these truths [truths consistent with Christian orthodoxy yet from non-Christian sources] from their unfortunate associations, take them away, and put them to their proper use for the proclamation of the gospel. . . . What else have many good and faithful people from amongst us done? . . . [expressing homage to the writings of Cyprian, Lactantius, Marius Victorinus, Optatus and Hilary of Poitiers] And look at how much the Greeks have borrowed! And before all of these, we find that Moses, that most faithful servant of God, had done the same thing: after all, it is written of him that "he was learned in all the wisdom of the Egyptians" (Acts 7:22).[23]

Medieval Developments

The relationship between faith and intellect continued into the medieval church, especially within the tradition of scholasticism. Anselm (eleventh century) described the necessity of faith and reason, not one or the other, asserting *fides quaerens intellectum* ("faith seeking understanding") and *credo ut intellegam* ("I believe in order that I may understand"). "His basic insight was that, while faith came before understanding, the content of that faith was nevertheless rational. These definitive formulae established the priority of faith over reason, just as they asserted the entire reasonableness of faith."[24]

But what kind of faith does the Christian need? Once again, the scholastics responded. As E. H. Klotsche summarizes, "The Schoolmen distinguished between *fides informis*, mere faith, and *fides formata caritate*, faith perfected in love. *Fides informis* may be *fides explicata*, explicit faith (faith with accurate knowledge of the church's doctrine), or *fides implicita*, implicit faith (readiness to believe whatever the church teaches). But it is only the *fides formata* which is meritorious and brings salvation."[25] However, it is Thomas Aquinas who describes, with a play on words, a threefold faith: *credere Deum, credere Deo, et credere in Deum* (believing truths about God, having a relationship with him, and being committed to and trusting him). "These are not three 'faiths,' but rather a threefold explanation of what it means that we have faith. Faith is a relationship in truth and trust, and we find our only proper rest as we adhere to the Living God. In faith, the whole rational self commits itself to the God who moves and calls us."[26]

The Reformation and Beyond

The early voices of the Reformation would echo many of these sentiments, expressing that faith possesses a rational component and that without it faith is wanting. For example, Calvin asserts that "faith rests not on ignorance, but on knowledge" of God and his will,[27] later explaining that one's knowledge of God rests on the Scriptures: "Take away the Word and no faith will then remain. . . . Now, therefore, we hold faith to be a knowledge of God's will toward us, perceived from his Word."[28] Scripture became a formative resource for faith, which was one of Luther's motives for putting the Bible into the vernacular of the people, preaching it as well as teaching it through catechism.[29]

More contemporary to modern times, John G. Stackhouse discusses the relationship between knowledge/reason and faith, pointing to the necessity of Scripture and theology for faith formation.

> This is the work of theology, and it is work every Christian must do: learning what God has said and learning how to say it for oneself in one's Christian community. The ignorance of the general public about the fundamentals of the Christian faith is regrettable. The ignorance of churchgoing Christians about the fundamentals of the Christian faith, however, is scandalous. Christians are somehow expected to think and feel and live in a distinctive way, as followers of Jesus, without being provided the basic vocabulary, grammar, and concepts of the Christian religion.[30]

Faith and reason are not epistemological contraries but coalesce in a Christian's life. Faith must be rational and reasonable, and formation relies on a constant engagement of the mind as one develops a distinctively Christian worldview fueled by the study of Scripture. Practically speaking, "A living faith is not a blind one. Engaging our heads means that our faith has to make sense to us on an intellectual level . . . going beyond wrestling with *whether* we believe to clarifying *what* we believe."[31]

What Is the Role of Experience in Faith Formation?

Throughout the church's history, theology has swung like a pendulum between the poles of intellect and experience, never to the exclusion of one but in terms of emphasis. This is in part because faith is more than orthodoxy—not just *fides* ("faith") but *fiducia* ("trust"). Faith must be more than *assensus*; it is not merely cognitive. "What is needed is not just the assent of one's mind but also the conversion of one's heart."[32]

However, when one begins to entertain the place of experience in faith and its formation, the impending danger of a return to the mystical Neoplatonism that arose in the early church looms large. The Reformation facilitated a reversal of most of the tenets of medieval Christianity, including rejecting a mystical ecstasy in favor of justification by grace through faith. But Lutheranism failed to fully embrace the experiential dimension of faith, degenerating into a faith of dry orthodoxy. Enter Pietism.[33]

The Pietist Tradition

Pietism, which began in Germany in the late sixteenth century, is one of the most influential and yet misunderstood traditions in the history of Christianity. Pietism is often characterized as a movement committed to devotional Bible study, small groups, and an experiential faith. For example, John L. Elias says, "The otherworldly Pietists . . . studied the Bible as God's revelation to the individual soul. . . . The Pietists favored living faith rather than chasing after an intellectual grasp of faith."[34] However accurate this description may be, it is also incomplete and too simplistic. It does not attend to the depth and the breadth of Pietism.

Pietism was built on the legacy of Luther's reform. According to F. Ernest Stoeffler, "The spiritual hunger grew in reaction to the coldness and formalism of the protestant state churches. Drawing from diverse roots, Pietism emerged as a quest to apply reformation doctrine to personal life." He notes Pietists' desire to facilitate new life by capturing "biblical models . . . motivated by the Spirit of Christ."[35] For example, rather than studying Scripture indirectly through church dogma, August Hermann Francke (1663–1727) and the Halle

School advanced a more direct approach to the study of Scripture. Pietism did not reject Luther's reformation but affirmed it—and in fact grew and matured from it. Through the work of the Wesleys, an Anglicized version of German Pietism arose in England: Methodism.

Word-Spirit Dynamic

A distinctive element of Pietism is the dynamic between the Spirit-inspired Word and the work of the Holy Spirit in the life, mind, and heart of the believer. All means of Bible reading would not be conducive to the formation of faith without the enlightenment or illumination of the Holy Spirit.

Philipp Jakob Spener (1635–1705), a German theologian and a leading figure in Pietism in the seventeenth century, compares those who study the Scriptures "by the illumination, witness, and sealing of the Holy Spirit" to those who have "acquired knowledge in their fields of study . . . with their own human efforts and without the working of the Holy Spirit." These people possess a mere intellectual knowledge of Scripture rather than knowing and experiencing God through the Scriptures.[36] He expresses that, apart from the Spirit, any Bible reading is pointless, and he concludes, "In such the reading of the Scriptures produces no effect. They attain only a natural knowledge of the letter of the Scriptures, without the inward power of the Spirit in them, and therefore by God's judgment can only become more hardened thereby and more incapable of the truth."[37]

Stoeffler observes, "In reading Scripture or hearing a sermon the worshipping believer is brought face to face with the revelatory activity of the divine Spirit, for the Word is God's means to communicate to a receptive human being his Law and Gospel."[38] Pietism affirmed that Scripture is God's revelation (as described by Lutheran theology) and that the Spirit illuminates and enlightens the life of the believer through Scripture; that is, the Scriptures are both a revelation and a means of revelation to the Christian. However, early Pietism avoided the extreme view of revelation apart from Scripture, viewing Scripture as a means of revelation and a guide to spiritual experience.

While some Pietists eventually gravitated into mysticism, this was never the intent of the Pietist tradition. Those who maintained a balance between academic and devotional study did not gravitate toward mysticism, but later generations of Pietists, who did not have the Lutheran theological background of Spener, Francke, Bengel, and Oetinger, did become "enthusiasts," as they were deemed.

In "On Hindrances to Theological Studies" (1680), Spener analyzes the differences between individuals he described as "enthusiasts," "mystics," and "radical" and the Pietist tradition.[39] His critique stems from the means by which one experiences the Holy Spirit. Spener affirms "the working presence of the Holy Spirit, the sealing, the illumination . . . the Spirit's consolation, the loving taste of eternal thing." However, he adds a caveat: "All these things are indicated in the Holy Scripture and are promised to believers and thus are not empty names and fantasies."[40] Spener regards enthusiastic mystics to be those who wanted the experience of the Spirit but without the use of the God-given instrument through which it may be experienced—that is, Scripture. He describes them as wanting to "rely on [their] own revelation" rather than God's revealed Word.[41]

Spener further asserts, "The mystics make use of strange words and manners of speech—many of them have no clear and precise way of thinking—one can separate these aside, as far as I am concerned, and attend to those which are clearer, revealed in the Holy Scriptures, and better represented by the experience of the pious."[42] Basically, the mystics of Spener's era wanted personal revelation and illumination—spiritual experience *without* the Word's guidance—while Pietists recognized that God's revelation precedes personal illumination and affirmed that genuine spiritual experience takes place *through* the Word.

Pietism shifted theological education "from dogmatic and institutional concerns toward existential issues in man's individual and corporate life."[43] However, this does not mean that theological education ceased to be academically inclined or theologically deep. Spener, in *Pia Desideria*, critiques the "unchristian academic life" prevalent in many "schools and universities" but affirms the potential for them to be reformed and "be recognized from the outward life of the students to be nurseries of the church for all estates and as workshops of the Holy Spirit."[44]

Given its understanding of Scripture and revelation and the polarizing alternatives of Lutheran orthodoxy and mysticism, Pietism became the believer's middle option, one that embraced the legitimacy of an experiential faith without slipping into mysticism and affirmed the orthodoxy of the Reformation. Pietism rested in the center of the academically inclined Lutheran tradition and the experientially motivated mystics/enthusiasts.

What Is the Relationship between Faith and Works in Faith Formation?

New words enter the English vocabulary on a routine basis. One of the newer additions to our vocabulary is *slacktivism*, meaning "the ideology for people who want to appear to be doing something for a particular cause without actually having to do anything such as posting on social media or 'liking' a post as actual activism."[45] Perhaps if he were here today, Dietrich Bonhoeffer would have picked up on this term when writing *The Cost of Discipleship* (1937), in which he articulated his concern about the prevailing and pervasive notion of "cheap grace," which focuses on salvation without an equivalent concern for discipleship. Cheap grace was (and continues to be) rampant in the American church.

What do slacktivism and cheap grace get wrong? That is, what is the relationship between faith and works, especially in regard to faith formation?

Faith is not equivalent to works, nor does the definition of saving faith somehow implicitly encompass works, although some even among evangelicals have endeavored to make it do so.[46] When the evangelist says, "All you have to *do* is believe!" this simply confuses the matter. Many have debated justification by faith alone (Paul in Romans and Galatians) versus justification by works (James 2). James 2:14–26 uses both *pistis* ("faith") and *pisteuō* ("believe"), which is key to understanding his apparent alternative to Paul's writings. James is focusing on the essential of *pisteuō*, "believing," and active faith versus merely affirming the content of faith. In this passage, he is saying that believing the faith statement, similar to the Shema of Deuteronomy 6:4, is insufficient; belief must be followed up with works.

But are we justified by faith alone or by works of faith? How does one reconcile Paul's gift of grace through faith apart from works with James's justification through faith with works? Jack Cottrell postulates the following solution:

> Faith has an *immediate and direct* relation to justification, since it is the only means that is compatible with justification as a free gift made available solely through the work of Jesus Christ. Thus says Paul. James's point, though, is that there is also a necessary indirect relation between works and justification, since true saving faith by its very nature will produce works, i.e., it will desire to obey and will seek to obey God's laws. Thus James can say that justification is by works, but only in a *secondary and indirect* sense insofar as works are the necessary expression of and evidence of faith. In summary, Paul's concern is to deny that justification is equally related to both faith and works, while James reminds us that works cannot be excluded from the picture since they are the inevitable result of faith—a point Paul himself makes in Rom 6:1ff.[47]

Both Paul and James affirm the value and the importance of works in terms of the natural result of a saving faith in Jesus Christ—a faith that should result in works (Eph. 2:8–10).

The matter of the relationship between faith and works continued throughout the church's history. The Latin Church captured the idea in the term *fiducia* ("trust"). "This is the crowning element of faith. Faith is not merely a matter of the intellect, nor of the intellect and emotions combined; it is also a matter of the will."[48] During the scholastic period, the notion of works was affirmed but kept separate from a saving faith.[49]

In the sixteenth century, Luther's desire to distance works from faith (and justification), often leading to the perception that good works have no value in the Christian life, led Philip Melanchthon to clarify Luther's position by affirming the value of good works in the Christian life, though not for justification.[50] Faith should always result in works—fruit—as a visible witness to transformation. According to contemporary authors Christopher Gehrz and Mark Pattie, service is formative to faith, and "a faith that makes sense in one's head and even brings warm sentiment to the heart is still not a living faith unless it makes a difference in how one lives."[51]

Is Faith and Its Formation Individual, Corporate, or Both?

Faith has a vertical dimension and a horizontal dimension. The vertical dimension involves a hermeneutical matter in Galatians regarding the nature of saving faith: "But the Scripture imprisoned everything under sin, so that the promise *by faith in Jesus Christ* might be given to those who believe. . . . For in Christ Jesus you are all sons of God, through faith" (Gal. 3:22, 26). The meaning of πίστεως Χριστοῦ (*pisteōs Christou*) in Paul (Rom. 3:22, 26; Gal. 3:22; Phil. 3:9) continues to be a subject of debate in Pauline scholarship. Should the genitive construction be understood objectively as "faith in Christ" or subjectively as "the faith(fulness) of Christ"?[52] The horizontal dimension involves the church. What is the value of the church, the community of faith and the body of Christ, in regard to faith, or does it have any influence?

Perhaps the best way to present this matter is in a diagram. It is typical to think about faith in this order: Christ→individual→church. Or perhaps in this order: Christ→church→individual. However, it may in fact be better

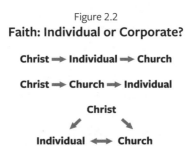

Figure 2.2
Faith: Individual or Corporate?

Christ ➡ Individual ➡ Church

Christ ➡ Church ➡ Individual

Christ
Individual ⬌ Church

Source: George Gordh, "The Concept of Corporate Faith," *Review and Expositor* 54, no. 1 (1957): 67–78.

illustrated by a triangle with Christ at the top and the individual and the church below, as demonstrated in figure 2.2.

There seems to be an undeniable link between individual faith and its formation within the community of the church. For example, the use of the Greek *allēlōn*, "one another," in the New Testament describes a dynamic within the Christian community, wherein faith is formed through "the interactions between and among members of the body of Christ."[53] Even the nature of Scripture itself seems to embolden the notion that the nurturing of faith is not intended to be a solo act but should be done in community. "Since Scripture has been understood to be formative beginning with the canonization process, congregations are to develop practices of Bible reading, Bible study, preaching, and worship that mirror such formative processes. When this shift in emphasis takes place, the church becomes the primary context within which Scripture functions to form and transform persons together as the people of God."[54]

Paul reminds Timothy, "I am reminded of your sincere faith, a faith that dwelt first in your grandmother Lois and your mother Eunice and now, I am sure, dwells in you as well" (2 Tim. 1:5). Leaders in the Puritan tradition understood that the Christian family, as part of the church, was the principal context for faith formation. Cotton Mather, a Puritan pastor, emphasized the corporate nature of faith within the Christian family without relinquishing personal responsibility.[55] Horace Bushnell's *Christian Nurture* (1846) asserts that faith is part of an organic relationship shared within families; faith originates with the parents and is mediated to the children through training. In more recent times, James Wilhoit's monumental work *Spiritual Formation as if the Church Mattered* (2008) underscores the necessity of the Christian community for faith formation.

Faith has both an individual and a corporate dimension.

| Conclusion

The basic questions regarding faith formation are indeed addressed by the great traditions that comprise the Christian faith. The origins of faith; how it grows in terms of intellect, experience, and volition; and the individual and cooperate nature of faith are all addressed by the two-thousand-year history of the faith. Leaning on Christian traditions and reappropriating them for the church in the twenty-first century provides a sound theological basis for the discussion of faith formation today.

| Discussion Questions

1. How does your own tradition describe faith and its formation?
2. What are the practical/pastoral implications for your understanding of faith formation?
3. Do the tenets of your theological tradition restrict what can be done to facilitate faith formation?
4. Do you and/or your tradition see faith as gifted or gained? Do you and/or your tradition emphasize intellect, experience, or volition? Individual or corporate faith?

| Further Reading

Bauerschmidt, Frederick Christian. *Thomas Aquinas: Faith, Reason, and Following Christ*. Oxford: Oxford University Press, 2013.

Cone, Steven D. *Theology from the Great Tradition*. New York: Bloomsbury T&T Clark, 2018.

Simpson, Christopher Ben. *Modern Christian Theology*. New York: Bloomsbury T&T Clark, 2016.

Stoeffler, F. Ernest. *German Pietism during the Eighteenth Century*. Studies in the History of Religions 24. Leiden: Brill, 1973.

3

Faith Formation Theory Revised

The study of faith formation is an area in ministry that has inspired much interest among practitioners and researchers seeking to understand a wide array of its functions in the Christian life. The topic has generated countless studies worldwide. While many of these studies are valuable, the groundbreaking study was published by James W. Fowler in 1981. In his book *Stages of Faith: The Psychology of Human Development and the Quest for Meaning*,[1] Fowler maps out the process by which people progress in faith. Using Jean Piaget's cognitive theory[2] as the core method of analysis, Fowler asserts that faith has a structure that can be described according to its developmental framework. While Fowler's theory is widely accepted as a universal framework for studying faith formation, it is important to recognize that his description of faith is quite different in character and content from anything evangelical Christians might experience in the spiritual life. Fowler's theory falls short of explaining how a Christian's faith grows. A new framework is needed for understanding faith formation among Bible-believing Christians who profess Jesus Christ as Lord and Savior.

This chapter, therefore, proposes a new model of faith formation based on a critical review of Fowler's theory and a framework of faith built from a qualitative study[3] of evangelical Christians.[4] This new perspective is based on the contention that faith formation encompasses the progressive dimension of Christian sanctification, involving spiritual conversion, renewal, and growth, facilitated by the rational (or schematic) and relational (or thematic) knowledge of biblical truth. In the process of faith formation, rational (or schematic) knowledge forms an *a priori* category of faith, and relational (or thematic) knowledge forms an *a posteriori* category of faith. The use of the Latin terms *a priori* ("what comes first" or "prior to") and *a posteriori* ("from what is after" or "subsequent to") in this chapter is limited to the epistemic character of knowledge. The term *a priori* denotes faith-forming knowledge that is acquired independent of experience, while the term *a posteriori* denotes faith-forming knowledge that is derived from experience.

Before proceeding, it is important to clarify the distinction between rational (or *schema*, σχῆμα) and relational (or *thema*, θέμα) dimensions of the human mind (see fig. 3.1). This understanding played a critical role in this study of faith formation. In general, the concept of schema represents the prototype of the rational mind that has a generative and normative power in the conception of analytical knowledge. It refers to the analytic-rational structure of the mind that serves as a starting point of and catalyst to learning. Schema signifies a high system of rationalist ideas that Gottfried Wilhelm Leibniz, Immanuel Kant, Frederic Bartlett, Jean Piaget, and Richard Anderson discussed in their epistemology. At the center of their assertion lies the objective nature of human conception. The concept of thema, on the other hand, represents the analytic-relational structure of the empirical mind that has a constructive and legitimating power in apprehending perceptual (or experiential) knowledge. It signifies a deep system of empiricist ideas that Aristotle, Immanuel Kant, William James, Lev S. Vygotsky, and Charles P. Peirce discussed in their epistemology. At the heart of thema theory is the objective nature of human perception or sense experience. In this study, both schematic and thematic perspectives of the human mind become the basic frameworks for understanding how evangelical Christians acquire knowledge and grow in faith.

Figure 3.1
Dimensions of the Human Mind

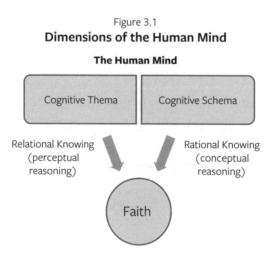

The Human Mind

| Cognitive Thema | Cognitive Schema |

Relational Knowing (perceptual reasoning)   Rational Knowing (conceptual reasoning)

Faith

Fowler's Faith Formation Theory Revisited

Some evaluative comments on Fowler's theory will be helpful in setting the stage to introduce a new model of faith formation. Keep in mind that this critical appraisal of Fowler's theory does not discredit his reputable work. His theory is a result of pursuing scholarly excellence, which deserves high recognition. No one would deny Fowler's epic achievement. However, his approach is theologically and theoretically inadequate for evangelical Christians, and their discussion of faith formation needs to go in a different direction.

Fowler proposes a framework for faith formation that parallels the structural model of human development. His faith stages, roughly correlated with age, are as follows (see table 3.1).

Stage 0: undifferentiated faith or pre-faith (birth to 2 years). The warm and nurturing environment provided by parents and primary caregivers creates toddlers' openness to trust God. Relying on Erik Erikson's psychosocial theory (1959), Fowler asserts that toddlers' pre-faith tendency is the by-product of early developmental experiences. For those who grew up in Christian homes, the undifferentiated faith stage is like a preconversion family experience in which positive parental nurture forms a pre-faith tendency or spiritual openness to believe in God later in life.

Stage 1: intuitive-projective faith (early childhood). According to Fowler, the faith of preschool-age children becomes highly intuitive in the sense that it is filled with a set of impressions and imaginations gained from early learning. Fowler believes that as children grow, their emotions and intuition have an extraordinary influence on their faith. Fowler also argues that preschool-age children are still unable to separate the content of faith from its context, meaning where faith is experienced. Children simply perceive faith in relation to the positive nurture they received from parents and caregivers. Intuitive-projective faith is mostly experience based.

Stage 2: mythic-literal faith (middle to late childhood). This stage typically is associated with elementary school children. As the abstract mind begins to form, they are capable of having a concrete faith (mythic-literal faith). Reasoning skills enable children to categorize their spiritual experience with a limited self-understanding and the perspectives of others. They can order their faith narratives and experiences based on the ideas of causality, fantasy, and reality. Mythic-literal faith is, however, still largely shaped by those who are important to children, such as parents, trusted adults, and friends. Their spiritual narratives, beliefs, and attitudes deeply affect children's faith during this stage.

Stage 3: synthetic-conventional faith (adolescence). This stage typically emerges in adolescence. Faith is shaped by abstract thinking and blossoms into certitude. While some physical and emotional issues arise and often interfere with adolescents' ability to reason, their abstract thinking ability causes their faith to become a lot more rational than before. While adolescents' viewpoints and values form the capacity for personal faith, they still affiliate their faith with the church or community of which they are a part.

Stage 4: individuative-reflective faith (early adulthood). This stage involves critically examining and internalizing faith. Young adult Christians critically examine the preestablished assumptions and traditions surrounding their spiritual experience and seek to legitimize their faith based on their personal beliefs and values. Overall, individuative-reflective faith is logical in terms of its makeup and applicability to reality.

Stage 5: conjunctive faith (middle adulthood). This stage is marked by the ability to embrace the complexities and ambiguities of faith. Personal reflection on life's meaning brings a deeper sense of purpose to middle adults' faith. While appreciating the value of community and others in faith formation, middle adults learn to personalize their faith based on individual self-reflection and take greater responsibility for what they truly believe.

Stage 6: universalizing faith (late adulthood). This stage of faith is marked by godly virtues such as humility, selflessness, justice, love, and compassion. Fowler believes that people rarely reach this final stage of faith, although he associates this stage with late adulthood. If we use biblical principles to interpret stage 6, this final stage is like reaching the end (*telos*) of faith formation, where Christians obtain full maturity in Jesus Christ.

Table 3.1
Fowler's Structural Model of Faith Formation

Stages	Characteristics
0. undifferentiated faith or pre-faith (birth to 2 years)	Parents' and primary caregivers' positive nurture creates a tendency for children to believe in God later in life.
1. intuitive-projective faith (early childhood)	Faith is infused with intuitions, impressions, and images.
2. mythic-literal faith (middle to late childhood)	Faith is influenced by children's concrete and literal knowledge.
3. synthetic-conventional faith (adolescence)	Faith is molded by abstract knowledge (e.g., logic, hypothesis).
4. individuative-reflective faith (early adulthood)	Faith is linked to critical knowledge (e.g., beliefs, values, third-person perspective taking, thesis, etc.).
5. conjunctive faith (middle adulthood)	Faith is embraced with its complexities and ambiguities (e.g., unknowns, mysteries, paradoxes, polarities, etc.).
6. universalizing faith (late adulthood)	Faith embodies godly virtues (e.g., love, charity, justice, prudence, selflessness, kindness, fortitude, etc.).

A Review of Fowler's Theory

While Fowler has exerted a great deal of scholarly influence, his theory has not been widely accepted in the evangelical church. Many evangelical Christians believe that Fowler's theory of faith formation is unscriptural and too mechanistic. It does in fact have theological and theoretical deficiencies; it is on these that the following critique will focus.

The theological framework that Fowler develops to explain faith formation is unscriptural and deeply problematic. Theologically speaking, Fowler's perspective on faith is fundamentally different from what the Bible teaches. Fowler understands faith as a "system of meaning" that people have for defining and sustaining life. He further asserts that such faith has form but no objective reference. Fowler simply assumes that faith is an existential human belief rather than the saving faith about which the Bible teaches. Fowler ignores the crucial theological tenets that make up and characterize the Christian faith. When studying faith formation, it is important to remember how the Bible defines faith. It says that faith is God's grace-induced and Spirit-empowered assent given in knowledge of, belief in, and trust in Jesus Christ (Matt. 19:11; Luke 1:16; 7:43; John 3:3–8; 16:8, 13; Acts 4:32; Rom. 1:28; 8:14; Gal. 5:10; Eph. 2:8; 2 Tim. 2:25; Heb. 3:14; 11:1; James 2:19). Under this perspective, Jesus is the content and the reference point in which faith is conceived, validated, and developed. He is the objective source of faith (John 8:32; 12:44; 14:6; Heb. 12:1–2). It is clear that Fowler overlooks the theological criteria of faith and falls short of explaining how the Christian faith forms and grows.

Furthermore, as a theoretical framework, Fowler's structural interpretation of faith being in a dyadic relationship with the rational mind (or schema) is far too limiting when applied to evangelical Christians' faith journey experiences. Based on the following assessment, it seems safe to argue that, in Fowler's framework, the dynamic dimension of relational knowledge (or thema), which gives faith its stability and resilience, is largely ignored, and faith is reduced to mere static knowledge. Relying heavily on Piaget's schematic perspective of cognition as a justificatory means, Fowler sees the rational consciousness as the primary means of faith formation. As a result, faith is confined to the analytic dimension of the human mind, and rational knowledge is enthroned as the singular determinant of faith formation. In regard to this perspective, we would naturally wonder what role, if any, relational knowledge (or thema)—the type of experiential knowledge we obtain from walking with Christ, serving the church, doing missionary work, practicing faith, etc.—plays in faith formation. As much as our faith grows through rational comprehension, it also grows through relational apprehension. Without the perceptual knowledge flooding our minds (or cognitive thema) via experience, our faith is only partial. Fowler fails to do justice to the relational dimension of the human mind in legitimating faith in the Christian life (see fig. 3.1).

Revising Faith Formation Theory: Rationale and Areas of Inquiry

As can be gleaned from this review of Fowler's theory, the upshot is the apparent need for a revised theory of faith formation. To address the theological and theoretical deficiencies noticed in Fowler's theory, the biblical and theoretical criteria of faith built from a qualitative study of evangelical Christians is used as the basic framework to examine the role that both rational (or schematic) and relational (or thematic) knowledge play in the formation of faith.

The author's (Jonathan's) study was based on a qualitative survey of 429 evangelical Christians in the United States, ranging in age from eighteen to sixty-six years old. As with many qualitative studies, the data analysis was complicated and took unexpected turns from its beginning to its end. Several hermeneutical techniques were used to analyze the data, but mostly the analysis involved grounded theory for identifying the schematic and thematic mechanisms behind faith-forming knowledge and experience. When distinct attributes of faith were observed in the data, the patterns of related attributes were analyzed, coded, and sorted into *a priori* and *a posteriori* categories of faith.

Following a series of analyses, theoretical saturation resulted in the identification of twenty-eight characteristics (or concepts) of faith. An inductive specification was then used to organize the twenty-eight characteristics into twelve elements (or categories) of faith. Based on further analysis, the twelve elements were grouped into four themes (or stages) of faith as follows: (1) converging faith: perceptive awareness and intuitive belief form an *a priori* category, and self-surrender forms an *a posteriori* category of faith; (2) consolidating faith: conceptual knowledge and ideological belief form an *a priori* category, and self-reformation forms an *a posteriori* category of faith; (3) conforming faith: prescriptive knowledge and systematic belief form an *a priori* category, and self-reinvigoration forms an *a posteriori* category of faith; and (4) contagious faith: evaluative knowledge and transformative belief form an *a priori* category, and selfless service forms an *a posteriori* category of faith.

Overall, the study findings indicate that the path of evangelical Christians' faith formation has both bidirectional and unidirectional movements (see fig. 3.2).[5] The movement between stages 1 and 2, which are considered the

Figure 3.2
An Evangelical Model of Faith Formation

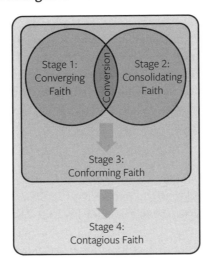

forerunners of faith formation, is bidirectional in that they synergistically refine one another and lead to stages 3 and 4 in a unidirectional manner. Please note that each stage builds on those preceding it except the first stage, which commences miraculously as a result of God's common grace if a person responds to his invitation of salvation. Furthermore, the faith qualities and characteristics that exist in a previous stage are embodied in a succeeding stage and are further refined into the higher attributes of faith.

Faith Formation Theory Revised: Toward an Evangelical Model of Faith Formation

This proposed model describes the stages of faith that undergird the spiritual life of evangelical Christians. This non-age-related framework contains four distinct faith stages, with each stage comprised of content, mental, and volitional elements. The content and mental elements belong to a rational (or schematic) dimension, and the volitional element belongs to a relational (or thematic) dimension of knowing (see table 3.2). While people obtain rational knowledge via comprehending scriptural concepts (i.e., abstract ideas), people gain relational knowledge via apprehending scriptural percepts (i.e., experiential ideas). It is through a synthesis of both rational and relational knowledge that faith grows, not just through rational (or schematic) knowledge alone, as Fowler contends.

Stage 1: Converging Faith

Converging faith represents the first stage of evangelical faith formation. God provides a perceptive awareness of his truth to the unsaved person based on his common grace, and such an awareness converges as the seedbed of saving faith when an intuitive belief causes the individual to surrender their life to God (Rom. 1:20). (Note: The word *faith* used in stage 1 refers to pre-faith or the seed of faith. Unless indicated otherwise, the word *faith* used in other sections of this chapter denotes the Christian faith, which was defined previously under the review of Fowler's theory.)

The converging faith stage belongs to the evangelism (or preconversion) phase of Christian discipleship in which the seed of faith sprouts as a result of a person having a limited understanding of God's revelation. Converging faith is inward oriented in that a person eventually learns to internalize the gospel and seeks to adopt the new way of life that Christ brings. As will be explained below, this stage is characterized by having perceptive awareness as content, intuitive belief as a propositional attitude, and self-surrender as the volitional act toward trusting God. Perceptive awareness and intuitive belief represent a rational (or schematic) means of knowing God, and the surrender of the self represents a relational (or thematic) means of knowing God. The union of these two means of knowing commences the converging faith to move forward.

Content Element: Perceptive Awareness

The perceptive awareness of God's truth represents the content element of converging faith. Perceptive awareness is a form of sensible knowledge of which a person has conscious awareness. This Spirit-enabled perception is a natural knowledge of God's goodness that does not involve a new spiritual nature. It is a reasonable awareness that invokes conviction among the unsaved and becomes a seedbed of saving faith later in life. In general, perceptive awareness is a form of knowledge that is concerned with perceiving or experiencing the whats of the Christian faith (e.g., perceptual facts).

In converging faith, perceptive awareness of God's truth represents a type of knowledge given to the unsaved from the outside. God, based on his common grace, provides sensible knowledge in a form of perception, whether direct or indirect, so that the unsaved can recognize the reality of his truth and presence (Rom. 1:19–20). Here the reader might wonder what "sensible knowledge" means since the Bible explicitly states the logical priority of regeneration over faith (Matt. 11:25–27; 16:17; John 3:3; 5:21; 6:44, 65; Eph. 1:4–5; 2:4–10; James 1:18). In the restricted sense, we are talking about the pre-faith knowledge of

God. Although the unsaved cannot apprehend God's revelation with their bare reason, the Holy Spirit momentarily removes their spiritual blindness and enables their minds to perceive his truth. With that being said, perceptual awareness comes in a form of subjective knowledge, and an additional understanding of the Bible is required for salvation (Rom. 10:14–15).

Mental Element: Intuitive Belief

Intuitive belief represents the mental element of converging faith. When perceptive awareness finds the adequacy of rational justification, it becomes a personally justified intuitive belief. This is a natural construal corresponding to the perceptive awareness that unsaved persons have about God. Intuitive belief is formed based on the key sensible inputs coming from the experiential understanding of God. While this form of belief remains in the realm of subjectivity and is highly symbolic, it still functions as a meaning-laden conviction toward belief in God.

In the Christian life, an intuitive belief becomes a preliminary form of conviction when the unsaved person becomes cognizant of God's truth (John 1:9; 14:26; 16:13). This is a type of belief that comes in the form of spiritual conviction (e.g., spiritual impression, prompting, and illumination). While intuitive belief may lack a cogent epistemic justification since it is formulated through a perceptual mental process and has sensible knowledge as its content, it still forms a pre-faith tendency toward trusting God.

Outcome: Self-Surrender

Self-surrender represents the volitional element of converging faith. Self-surrender represents an inner disposition of the unsaved person toward God that comes in a form of commitment (John 3:3–8; 16:8; 2 Tim. 2:25). It is a conscious acknowledgment of God that is based on an inner response to the ministry of the Holy Spirit (John 16:8).

Theologically speaking, self-surrender is equivalent to repentance. It represents a change of heart, which results in the rejection of sin and the old way of life. In converging faith, both the encompassing act of God through the agency of the Spirit and the active involvement of human agency through personal decision are required (Rom. 10:9). While the work of the Spirit operative in human beings is the fundamental cause of self-surrender, unbelievers must respond to God with a personal decision. It is the Spirit-enabled human will that causes the unsaved person to totally surrender their life to God. This allegiance of the human soul to God coming in a form of repentance is the highest expression of the human will that unites the unsaved person to their Creator (Rom. 10:9).

Stage 2: Consolidating Faith

Consolidating faith represents the second stage of evangelical faith forma-tion. This stage belongs to the establishment phase of Christian discipleship, in which a solid foundation of faith is laid. Consolidating faith is downward oriented in that as a person conforms to the image of Christ, they lay a deep spiritual root in the certitude of salvation and the ownership of faith. As will be explained below, this stage is characterized by having conceptual knowledge as content, ideological belief as a propositional attitude, and self-reformation as the outcome of volitional consent. In the life of faith, conceptual knowledge and ideological belief represent a rational (or schematic) means of knowing God, and the reformation of the self represents a relational (or thematic) means of knowing God. A synthesis of these two means of knowing brings forth consolidating faith.

Content Element: Conceptual Knowledge

The conceptual knowledge of God's truth represents the content element of consolidating faith. Conceptual knowledge is a form of descriptive knowl-edge that is concerned with grasping systematic relations in the meaning of ideas. In learning, meanings are organized in clusters to form a significant unit of thought.

In faith formation, conceptual knowledge is concerned with understanding systematic relations in the meaning of biblical ideas. This process involves an *a priori* necessity of inference, which means understanding a set of interrelated scriptural concepts based on semantic analysis and inductive generalization. As an example, when a person learns certain scriptural ideas about God's holiness, humans' inability to satisfy God's perfect justice, and Christ's sac-rificial death on the cross for humankind, the conceptual knowledge about propitiation—the word that explains an idea of appeasement required by God's perfect justice (Rom. 3:24–26; Heb. 2:17)—will emerge in their mind. Conceptual knowledge is about having this capacity to reason and assimilate multiple ideas based on their semantic relations. This process results in know-ing the whats of scriptural ideas (e.g., conjectural facts).

Mental Element: Ideological Belief

Ideological belief represents the mental element of consolidating faith. When clusters of conceptual knowledge turn into the content of justified belief, a network of ideas emerges as a personal system of credos called ideo-logical belief. This belief system, which is particular and subjective, then acts as explanatory principles to guide faith in its formation process.

Practically speaking, an ideological belief is like a system of values or the inner standards of faith to which a person adheres. As a collection of normative tenets, an ideological belief accounts for rational action established on the ground of personal understanding and assurance. While converging faith in its most rudimentary form may not include ideological beliefs, consolidating faith cannot function without an ideological system of beliefs forming a credence framework for spiritual life. Overall, an ideological belief provides a pathway for bridging faith and life (2 Cor. 5:7; Titus 2:2).

Outcome: Self-Reformation

Self-reformation represents the volitional element of consolidating faith. Self-reformation is the outward evidence of assimilating conceptual knowledge and ideological belief into one's Christian life. Such a change is not limited to mere behavioral modification; it also involves a sudden event of conversion that is followed by a gradual process of renovation. During this process, a person learns to realign their entire being to the truth made known to them by the Holy Spirit. How they view reality, truth, and value changes as a result.

Theologically speaking, the reformation of the self is equivalent to conversion, in which the entire self is restructured and reformulated according to the truth of the Bible. It involves a change of the entire human nature. First, it involves a change of mind. The mind is set not on earthly things but on the things of God (Rom. 8:5–6; Phil. 3:19; Col. 3:2). It is filled with God's Word, infused with the Spirit's enlightenment, and renewed in Christ (Rom. 8:5–6; 12:2). Second, self-reformation entails a change of emotion. How a person feels about God, others, and self changes. This process involves correcting and reorganizing the habits of emotional encounters in life. And third, self-reformation involves a change of will. One's inclination, aspiration, and intent become Christ centered and cause a person to walk in the direction that God provides in life.

Stage 3: Conforming Faith

Conforming faith represents the third stage of evangelical faith formation. This stage represents the equipping phase of Christian discipleship. Conforming faith is upward oriented in that it propels a person into the vertical spiral of spiritual maturity. As will be explained below, this stage is characterized by having prescriptive knowledge as content, systematic belief as a propositional attitude, and self-reinvigoration as the outcome of volitional consent. In the Christian life, prescriptive knowledge and systematic belief represent a rational (or schematic) means of knowing God, and the reinvigoration of the self represents a relational (or thematic) means of knowing God. The appropriate integration of these two means of knowing produces conforming faith.

Content Element: Prescriptive Knowledge

The prescriptive knowledge of God's truth represents the content element of conforming faith. This form of knowledge is concerned with understanding the relationship among intrinsic parts of ideas and explaining their associations based on a legitimating criterion that is functional in nature. In conforming faith, prescriptive knowledge focuses on the procedural output, or the hows of knowing. It values knowing "what it ought to be" rather than "what it is" in the Christian life.

Theoretically speaking, prescriptive knowledge is outward oriented in that it legitimates faith through action. When the tenets behind perceptual and conceptual knowledge are accommodated in learning, they become an organized set of precepts at a varying level of generality. This type of knowledge, in turn, functions as a rule of action to guide faith in the Christian life.

There are two forms of prescriptive knowledge: intrarelational and interrelational. Since both forms arise in an imperative manner and guide the life of faith, it is difficult to distinguish their meanings. However, the basic difference is in their aim. Intrarelational precepts focus on instilling order to a person's inner life with God, whereas interrelational precepts focus on bringing a relational harmony with others. For example, in the Bible, divine counsels (Pss. 16:7–8; 73:24; Prov. 19:20; John 14:26; 16:13; James 3:17) and divine commands (Exod. 20:3–17; Matt. 22:34–40; John 14:15, 21; 15:10, 14; Rom. 2:15; 7:7–11; Gal. 2:21; 1 John 2:3–5; 2 John 1:6) represent these two forms of prescriptive knowledge, respectively. While divine counsels are intrarelationally directed at strengthening one's relationship with God, divine commands are interrelationally directed at strengthening one's relationship with others. Overall, prescriptive knowledge is indispensable to a good life of faith. It results in gracious character and is practicable in its orientation. Prescriptive knowledge informs the individual and renders them able to live out what they know in Jesus Christ.

Mental Element: Systematic Belief

Systematic belief represents the mental element of conforming faith. Systematic belief is a coherent structure of tenets that provides epistemic normativity to faith. It is a form of fundamental conjecture that converges when the propositions underlying prescriptive constructs are extrapolated into a system of thoughts. Such a belief is prima facie, meaning justified by the initial reasoning until a higher order of inferential justification replaces it. This type of conjecture involves a doxastic decision and positions itself as a set of implicit inferences and develops into philosophical and theological tenets in the Christian life. Compared to ideological belief, which is particular and subjective, systematic belief tends to be systematic and objective in its composition.

Theologically speaking, systematic belief represents a set of axioms that guides faith formation. It is equivalent to the personal dogma that individuals theorize from prescriptive knowledge. Implicitly or explicitly, such a set of beliefs functions as the standard of cognition and behavior that provides the norms to faith. Then according to the set of norms created, faith evolves with epistemic competence and consistency so that it may grow in conformity to biblical standards.

Outcome: Self-Reinvigoration

Self-reinvigoration represents the volitional element of conforming faith. Self-reinvigoration refers to the cathartic impact of accommodating prescriptive knowledge and systematic belief in the Christian life. This process is highly transformative in that it solidifies faith, provides fresh vigor to the soul, and increases the will for vibrant Christian living. This inward change allows the believer to engage in a deeper relationship with God and experience self-rejuvenation.

The effect of accommodating prescriptive knowledge and systematic belief in the Christian life is like that of the Pentecost phenomenon (Acts 2:1–47). It is much more than merely learning new information or having a convincing belief. It represents receiving Spirit-empowered knowledge, belief, and capacity for righteous living. This is where the Holy Spirit finds the believer in their humble state of obedience, enlightens their mind, and guides their actions. As a result, faith is renewed and rejuvenated deep within.

Stage 4: Contagious Faith

Contagious faith represents the fourth and final stage of evangelical faith formation. This stage belongs to the entrusting or service phase of Christian discipleship. Contagious faith is outward oriented in that it causes a person to move forward and to live a life of missions. As will be explained below, this stage is characterized by having evaluative knowledge as content, transformative belief as a propositional attitude, and selfless service as the outcome of volitional consent. Evaluative knowledge and transformative belief represent a rational (or schematic) means of knowing God, and selfless service represents a relational (or thematic) means of knowing God. The synthesis of these two means of knowing results in the formation of contagious faith.

Content Element: Evaluative Knowledge

The evaluative knowledge of God's truth represents the content element of contagious faith. Evaluative knowledge is the foundational certainty of thoughts. It builds itself on a corpus of inductive investigations and the accommodating of scriptural principles into one's mind. Unlike prescriptive knowledge, which is outward oriented and legitimates faith through its output, evaluative knowledge is inward oriented and legitimates faith by establishing principle-based criteria as the foundational property of faith. In general, evaluative knowledge is associated with knowing the whys of the Christian faith (John 14:6; Acts 4:12; 1 Cor. 15:14, 17; Eph. 2:8–9; 2 Tim. 1:12; Heb. 6:19).

In the Christian life, evaluative knowledge functions as pre-justified knowledge that governs the inclusion and exclusion of newly acquired information. If a new idea coheres with and corresponds to the existing structure of evaluative knowledge, it is accommodated and ends up reconfiguring the existing content property of faith. Theoretically speaking, evaluative knowledge is equivalent to the foundational content of faith or so-called meta-knowledge. Evaluative knowledge operates as the critical criteria for assimilating and accommodating new knowledge to faith.

Mental Element: Transformative Belief

Transformative belief represents the mental element of contagious faith. As an individual accommodates intuitive, ideological, and systematic beliefs into a meaningful structure of thoughts, these assimilated beliefs produce a meta-system of belief. This newly formed belief system is transformative belief. Transformative belief is like having a belief about beliefs. It functions as the deep-seated ideological map that guides the operation of other beliefs.

As a theory of knowledge, transformative belief represents the base of all beliefs. Transformative belief denotes the meta-level structure of certainty that has been fully justified at the core of one's consciousness. Unlike the three other beliefs, transformative belief functions as the ultra-system of all beliefs. While intuitive, ideological, and systematic beliefs operate as the mental representations of faith at the outer level, transformative belief operates at the inner core of one's consciousness. In general, transformative belief represents the foundational schematic system of thought that only changes when a person goes through a profound paradigm shift. In life, transformative belief functions as the backbone of all thoughts. It operates above and beyond our everyday thinking.

Outcome: Selfless Service

Selfless service represents the volitional element of contagious faith. A glimpse of complete faith in Jesus Christ inspires a person for selfless service at this stage of spiritual growth. Selfless service signifies the faith that has been fully transformed by Christ and that is being lived out under the power of the Spirit. Reaching this stage of faith requires an individual to embody the character and mission of Jesus Christ. Though the completion of faith formation is not attainable on this earth and remains distant in heaven, its aptness and potential for completion are still present. This possibility is translated into a perpetual expansion of God's love embodied in selfless service. In general, contagious faith prompts selfless service, as selfless service legitimates contagious faith through action.

The volitional element of contagious faith has two qualities that complement each other in action. The inner quality of contagious faith is characterized by embodying the agape love of Jesus Christ (Rom. 4:25; 2 Cor. 5:15). This results from a deep realization of his selfless character and servanthood. Naturally, a person of contagious faith finds an inner pleasure in being like Christ because they are under the influence of Christ's character, sacrifice, and benevolence. The outer quality of contagious faith is characterized by living a life of mission. The person of contagious faith understands that faith is not just a matter of knowing God's truth or becoming altruistic. It is state of being with Christ by serving him and others. Such a relationship requires the believer to become part of God's kingdom force, spreading the good news and living a life of mission (Matt. 28:18–20; Mark 12:30–31; John 15:12–14; Gal. 2:20; Phil. 2:4). Since the Christian life is rooted in the missional nature of Christ (Mark 10:45; Phil. 2:5–8; 1 Tim. 2:6), a person of contagious faith learns to influence the world for Christ by fully participating in the command of the Great Commission. Such is the Christ-honoring pathway toward completing one's faith formation.

Table 3.2
Summary of Evangelical Faith Formation Stages

Stages of Faith	Dimensions of Knowing	Elements of Faith	Qualities/Characteristics
Stage 1: CONVERGING faith	Rational dimension	Perceptive awareness	Is infused with perceptive awareness (e.g., spiritual perception) (subjective abstraction, tied to a personal situation)
			Involves knowing the perceptive whats of Christian faith
		Intuitive belief	Is inward oriented
			Is based on the assimilation of spiritual percepts
			Is primarily intuitive in its belief structure
	Relational dimension	Self-surrender	Belongs to the evangelism phase of discipleship
			Leads to the surrender of the self
Stage 2: CONSOLIDATING faith	Rational dimension	Conceptual knowledge	Is infused with the conceptual knowledge that is descriptive in nature (low-level abstraction, tied to an individual context)
			Involves knowing the conceptual whats of Christian faith
		Ideological belief	Is downward oriented
			Is based on the assimilation of scriptural concepts
			Is primarily categorical in its belief structure
	Relational dimension	Self-reformation	Belongs to the establishment phase of discipleship
			Leads to the reformation of the self
Stage 3: CONFORMING faith	Rational dimension	Prescriptive knowledge	Is infused with the prescriptive knowledge that is functional in nature (high-level abstraction, tied to multiple contexts)
			Involves knowing the hows of Christian faith
		Systematic belief	Is upward oriented
			Is based on the accommodation of scriptural precepts
			Is primarily precept centered in its belief structure
	Relational dimension	Self-reinvigoration	Belongs to the equipping phase of discipleship
			Leads to the reinvigoration of the self

Stages of Faith	Dimensions of Knowing	Elements of Faith	Qualities/Characteristics
Stage 4: CONTAGIOUS faith	Rational dimension	Evaluative knowledge	Is infused with the evaluative knowledge that is principle based (meta-level abstraction, meta-contextual)
			Involves knowing the whys of Christian faith
		Transformative belief	Is outward oriented
			Is based on the accommodation (or divergence) of scriptural principles
			Is primarily principle based in its belief structure (e.g., meta-theory)
	Relational dimension	Selfless service	Belongs to the entrusting (i.e., service) phase of discipleship
			Leads to the missional life of service

| Conclusion

This chapter set out to introduce a new model of faith formation due to theological and theoretical deficiencies in Fowler's faith formation theory. It revealed that the proper integration of both rational (or schematic) and relational (or thematic) knowledge forms and grows faith.

Based on this chapter, the following conclusions about faith formation can be drawn. First, the instrumental cause of faith formation is attributed to knowing, believing, and trusting God. However, the primary cause, as indicated by evangelical Christians, is God, who brings atonement to humanity through the work of Jesus Christ. Both instrumental and primary causes correspond to the commencement and development of faith among evangelical Christians. Second, faith formation is a spiritual phenomenon that is affixed to the complex interworking of the Holy Spirit, the rational mind (i.e., cognitive schema), and the relational mind (i.e., cognitive thema). It is the union of these spiritual-intellectual forces that generates faith when an individual responds to God in Christ (John 6:44; Rom. 1:8; 8:14; Eph. 2:8–10; Phil. 3:10–11; Heb. 11:1; 12:2; James 2:26; 1 John 2:14; Jude 3). Third, evangelical Christians go through the stages of faith formation in a nonmechanical fashion, with each stage building on the content, mental, and volitional elements of faith developed in previous stages, except for the first stage, which results from the conscious awakening of the human soul made possible by God's grace. In each stage, the content and mental elements of faith serve as a rational (or schematic) means of knowing God, and the volitional element serves as a relational (or thematic) means of knowing God.

The model of faith formation proposed in this chapter is still in an incipient stage and needs further development. However, the need to address this important topic in the context of research is important. In the near future, it will be important to replicate the same study with a different Christian population to see how their faith-forming knowledge and experience correspond to the four stages described in this chapter. Such a study will be valuable in validating the model proposed in this chapter.

Discussion Questions

1. How would you define *faith*? How does faith grow?
2. What are your impressions of Fowler's theory of faith formation? Evaluate Fowler's faith stages based on your theological belief.
3. What is the relationship between knowledge and faith formation? How has your knowledge of the Bible formed your faith?
4. What relationship exists between experience and faith formation?
5. Evaluate the evangelical model of faith formation proposed in this chapter. What do you agree or disagree with?
6. How has the ministry of your local church informed and transformed your faith?
7. Who was instrumental in passing the Christian faith on to you? In what ways was that person effective?

Further Reading

Estep, James R., and Jonathan H. Kim. *Christian Formation: Integrating Theology and Human Development*. Nashville: B&H Academic, 2010.

Fowler, James W. *Stages of Faith: The Psychology of Human Development and the Quest for Meaning*. New York: HarperCollins, 1981.

Hagberg, Janet O., and Robert A. Guelich. *The Critical Journey: Stages in the Life of Faith*. Salem, WI: Sheffield, 1995.

Saucy, Robert L. *Minding the Heart: The Way of Spiritual Transformation*. Grand Rapids: Kregel, 2013.

Wilcox, Mary M. *Developmental Journey: A Guide to the Development of Logical and Moral Reasoning of Social Perspective*. Nashville: Abingdon, 1979.

Wilhoit, James C. *Spiritual Formation as if the Church Mattered: Growing in Christ through Community*. Grand Rapids: Baker Academic, 2008.

4

A Critique of Faith
Development Theory

J ames Fowler's faith development theory, as outlined in his book *Stages of Faith* (1981), has experienced widespread dissemination and has shaped research in faith development both in the United States and worldwide. The Center for Research in Faith and Moral Development at Emory University, which seeks to provide empirical research on faith development, has helped to elevate the field of study.

It has been almost forty years since *Stages of Faith* was published. In the eighties and nineties, Fowler's theory influenced research in the areas of practical theology, pastoral counseling, and worship. For example, Jeff Astley and Leslie Francis edited a book, *Christian Perspectives on Faith Development*, that asserts that Fowler's theory provides the church with a powerful incentive to reconceptualize aspects of ministry and mission.[1] Fowler's more recent works, *Pastoral Care and Faith Development* (1987) and *Weaving the New Creation: Stages of Faith and the Public Church* (1991), address specific aspects of faith development. These works and others continue to make a connection between faith development theory and the practice of ministry, particularly within the field of Christian religious education. As expressed throughout this book, Fowler's theory of faith development continues to significantly impact how Christian religious educators understand the psychological aspects of faith formation.

While the benefits of Fowler's faith development theory are evident, over the decades, a number of critiques have emerged. Chapter 3 attempts to provide a revised view of Fowler's faith development theory based on an evangelical perspective of faith formation. The chapter shows that faith without an *a priori* justification coming from the conceptual understanding of scriptural truth is hollow, and faith without an *a posteriori* legitimation deriving from the experiential understanding of scriptural truth is blind. The proper integration of both rational (or schematic) and relational (or thematic) knowledge forms and grows faith.

Building on chapter 3, this chapter provides a detailed analysis of some of the primary critiques of Fowler's theory. This isn't an exhaustive treatment; rather, particular focus is given to the following aspects of faith formation: the content and structure of faith, structuralism, and gender and ethnic diversity.

Critique of Fowler's Faith Development Theory

The Content and Structure of Faith

In the field of Christian religious education, Fowler's theory of the content of faith has been critiqued by evangelicals, mainline Christians, and even universalists.[2] Timothy Paul Jones states that evangelical Christian educators have questioned the compatibility of Fowler's understanding of faith with an evangelical view of faith. He suggests that these critiques fall into two camps: (1) studies regarding the relationship between content and structure in the Christian faith and (2) studies related to the relationship between Fowler's understanding of faith as a universal developmental structure and a Christian understanding of faith as a divine gift.[3]

In regard to the primary content of faith, Fowler makes a distinction between religious faith and human faith.[4] Fowler's theory of human faith is not to be confused with religious faith. Faith is interactive and social and requires a community and nurture. Human faith, for Fowler, is a patterned process by which we find meaning.[5] Thus, for Fowler, faith is "the way people understand and experience faith emerging through predictable stages."[6] In other words, faith is the way people make meaning out of life. It is important to acknowledge that when Fowler is talking about faith, he is talking about human faith not religious faith.

Fowler offers a structural-developmental view of faith that includes self, others, and shared centers of value and power.[7] Here faith is a way of knowing that does not require assent to a specific knowledge.[8] Fowler's view of faith is influenced by Wilfred Cantwell Smith, who draws a sharp distinction between faith and belief. For Smith, belief involves assenting intellectually to concepts or propositions as set forth in religious doctrines and creeds.

If concentration is given toward belief, then the various religious traditions recognize their differences. Smith states that the meaning of belief in a premodern world was based on a personal or subjective engagement that did not demand any assertions of belief.[9] Faith calls attention to the similarities among faith traditions, while beliefs divide. For Smith, faith is "a quality of the person not the system."[10] For Fowler, faith involves "an orientation of the total person, giving purpose and goal to one's hopes and strivings, thoughts and actions."[11] According to Fowler, "Faith rather than belief or religion is the most fundamental category in the human quest for relation to transcendence. . . . Faith, it appears, is generic, a universal feature of human living, recognizably similar everywhere despite the remarkable variety of forms and contents of religious practice and belief."[12] He states, "Faith combines a phenomenological account of what faith *does*, with a conceptual model of what faith *is*. Faith is deeply related to the human need to find and make meaning, and to do so in a trusting relation to the divine Being and Spirit from whom creation issues."[13] A person's or group's faith is only part of belief. Faith includes unconscious dynamics as well as conscious awareness. It includes deep emotions and cognitive operations and content. Faith is more personal and more existential than belief, as understood in modernity.[14]

A Christian View of Faith

For many Christians who believe that Scripture is a means of authority for faith and practice, Fowler's (and Smith's) view of faith raises concerns. Christians assent to specific content with the act of faith, particularly as reflected in the self-revelation of Jesus Christ. In other words, what defines a Christian is their affirmation of belief, reflected in the historical creeds and in sacred Scripture. A Christian view of faith includes belief (orthodoxy), practice (orthopraxis), and the heart (orthopathy). Smith's influence on Fowler results in a view of faith that does not include assent to specific content of faith.[15]

While Christians may not accept the content of Fowler's view of faith, as developed from Smith's thesis, this does not mean that Fowler's faith development theory has no relevance for Christian religious educators. While Fowler's structural-developmental view of faith development does not address Christian faith, it may address how people go through stages of faith.

Fowler is concerned that the meaning of faith, or the content of faith, will be misunderstood by Christians because he views faith from a human perspective. His view of faith does not deny claims made by Christians or other religious people that faith is a human response to God's grace and that faith is a gift of God.[16] Rather, Fowler develops his stages of faith as a way to study faith as the formation of persons' ways of relating to their neighbors, themselves, and their world in light of their images of an ultimate reality. He views faith from a psychological perspective not from a theological perspective.[17] He separates the content of faith from psychological factors that facilitate the operation of faith within the personality (i.e., cognitive, affective, and social domain).[18]

He is less concerned about the *content* of faith and more concerned about the *structure* of how people shape faith and integrate their worldviews; he does not allow the *content* of orthodox faith to be determined.[19] Fowler recognizes that faith can be open to others and to the transcendent, which is reflected in his view that faith is a person's or a community's "way-of-being-in-relation to an ultimate environment." While this ultimate reality is not consistent with a Christian view of faith, it does suggest that Fowler is open to a transcendent realm. Christian religious educators can follow Fowler's structure of faith as a "psychical context by which Christian faith is affected but by which Christian faith development remains distinguishable."[20] What Fowler means by "psychical context" is the psychological dimensions of faith, but Christian faith is different.

James Loder: Convictional Knowing

James Loder, a contemporary of Fowler and former professor of Christian education at Princeton Theological Seminary, proposes an alternative approach to faith development theory in his book *The Transforming Moment* (1981). Loder and Fowler engage in critical dialogue regarding each of their books and provide careful critiques of each other's theories. Loder's primary concern centers around the meaning of faith as reflected in Scripture and church history and the role the Holy Spirit plays in human transformation.[21] Rather than arguing for a series of stages through which all people move, he focuses on what he calls "convictional knowing," life-changing events through which ways of knowing, believing, feeling, and acting are radically altered. In *The Transforming Moment*, Loder gives a theological rationale for human transformation in his five-stage "logic" of the human spirit. The logic of transformation occurs in a series of consequential steps in which there is continuity and discontinuity. The steps include the following:

1. *Conflict.* Conflict occurs whenever there is discontinuity in a person's lived world. It may be an adverse incident such as an accident, an illness, the loss of a loved one, or a sense of restlessness that threatens the community or stability of the person's lived world. The conflict provokes painful anxiety.

2. *Interlude for scanning.* The self cannot live with this painful anxiety since it is not comfortable with not knowing. Therefore, it begins scanning for possible ways to resolve the conflict and reduce the anxiety level. The scanning may involve conscious and unconscious acts occurring concurrently. This period of scanning may last a moment or years.

3. *Insight.* A solution is provided, which may not be due to logical reasoning but to a constructive act of imagination. Two or more noncompatible solutions may come together to produce a workable resolution to the conflict. This is the key process in transformation.

4. *Release.* The appearance of the solution, sometimes known as the aha moment, is accompanied by a release of energy, which is the response of the unconscious and reduces the anxiety level. Simultaneously, there is the opening of the knower to new and expanded knowing or consciousness. This opening is a response of the conscious mind. Knowing is expanded by this opening, resulting in a transformed lived world in which the person is able to see things clearer than before. It involves renewal in self-identity and relationship to the lived world.

5. *Interpretation/verification.* In this final stage, the person uses their transformed knowing to rebuild or improve their lived world. In reworking their life forward, which Loder calls "correspondence," the person now lives with a renewed sense of identity and purpose. In reworking backward, or "congruence," the person is able to understand their past experiences in a new light because of their new understanding.[22]

Loder argues that transformation occurs both within and across the life span and that it reflects a relational framework for the work of the Holy Spirit both within creation and through redemptive engagement.

Loder moves beyond Fowler's generic understanding of human faith to give focus to the dynamics of Christian transformation. Loder develops his theology from a Chalcedonian Christology that emphasizes the divine and human aspects of Jesus Christ. Loder believes that through this transformational process, the human spirit is reconstructed by the work of the Holy Spirit. The logic of convictional knowing permeates every aspect of human development as a pattern that governs the transition process.[23] This process of transformation takes place in a variety of life experiences. Loder's description of the impact of the Holy Spirit on human transformation provides Christian religious educators with a credible alternative to Fowler's *content* and *structure* of faith development.

Structuralism

Fowler's faith development is in the constructive-developmental family of Jean Piaget's cognitive development theory and particularly Lawrence Kohlberg's moral development theory. Piaget, the Swiss genetic epistemologist, argues that people developing logical abilities move in describable, sequential stages from infancy into early adulthood. Kohlberg researches the logic of moral decision-making in an attempt to make educators aware of the implications of moral development for teaching. Also, Erik Erikson's psychosocial stages of development give focus to a stage-based model of adult psychosocial development, which concludes that as adults deal with crisis, they move from stage to stage.

In all of these developmental theories, stages are seen as universal and sequential. Individuals must move through a particular stage before they can enter the next stage. The early stages give focus to maturation, while the later stages give focus to an individual's interaction with the environment. Fowler's faith development theory is an attempt to show how individuals move through stages of faith in order to make meaning.

Kohlberg was a colleague of Fowler and influences his constructive-development perspective. Fowler writes, "My initial excitement about Kohlberg's work provided an impetus to try to operationalize a rich concept of faith and to begin to look more systemically at faith in a constructive-development perspective."[24] Fowler adapts Piaget's and Kohlberg's constructive-development approach to stage development that focuses on cognition and moral reasoning. The constructive-development approach emphasizes stage development theory.

Fowler's structuralist approach can be confusing because, on the one hand, he follows Piaget's structuralist approach by giving focus to cognition (structures of knowing), but on the other hand, he widens the scope of universalizing faith to include aspects of relationships (ego/personality development).[25] Fowler does not develop a stage theory based on the nature of transcendence and the development of the self but relies on Reinhold Niebuhr's theology for a traditional view of God. It is here that Fowler differs from Kohlberg.[26] Kohlberg's theory is based on facts or knowledge and does not provide space for values or human emotions.[27] Fowler's concern is echoed in more recent studies in social psychology that argue against a cognitive basis for moral development and give focus to the affective aspects of morality.[28] Even with this distinction regarding Fowler's more affective focus compared to Kohlberg's more cognitive approach, it is important to point out that Fowler's theory is based on a structuralist approach to stage development. While giving attention to the affection domain of faith development, Fowler still overstresses the rational aspects, particularly when it comes to empirical data.[29]

Gender and Ethnic Diversity

It is not surprising that Fowler is criticized for not including more gender and ethnic diversity in his research sample, since most of the research participants used to formulate the cognitive-structuralist theories were white males, with only some women. The lack of gender and ethnic diversity was, and continues to be, a major concern in theological education. Maria Harris indicates that in the field of Christian religious education, some strides have been made regarding ethnic diversity, particularly with Latinos/as, but there is a long way to go. She goes on to say that religious educators are becoming more attentive to the vast range of approaches people take to the same religious story.[30] She says that "white religious educators are examining white privilege and power. We who are white are learning—or trying to learn—our own biases, and working more carefully not to assume that our way is the right or only way."[31] This lack of diversity is reflected in North American theological education in general and in particular in seminaries accredited by the Association of Theological Schools (ATS), where Fowler did his research.[32]

While Fowler argues that his faith development research involved 359 subjects, consisting of equal numbers of females and males, he, along with Kohlberg, continues to be criticized for a lack of gender equality in his studies.[33] Kohlberg's colleague Carol Gilligan, in her book *In a Different Voice* (1993), challenges the cognitive-structuralist approach by arguing that women make moral decisions based on the "ethic of care," or relationships, while men focus on logic and reason.[34] In moral development theory, Kohlberg uses the classic Heinz dilemma to determine whether Heinz should steal the drug or not. Young boys indicated that Heinz should steal the drug because if he doesn't, his wife will die. A young woman, Amy, indicated that he should not steal the drug because even if he saves his wife's life, he would go to jail if caught.[35] While males structure moral decisions on the basis of fairness and justice, females focus on responsibility and care.[36]

Gilligan's research focuses on a different core of moral reasoning, which accounts for women's low scores on Kohlberg's interview measure. For Gilligan, the ethic of care resolves moral dilemmas by deciding how care and responsibility are called for in a given situation. Gilligan reframes women's psychological development as focused on a struggle for connection rather than achieving separation and autonomy, as Kohlberg develops. She replaces the hierarchy of rights with a web of relationships and articulates an ethic of responsibility that stems from an awareness of interconnection.

In the same family as Gilligan and Jean Baker Miller,[37] the book *Women's Ways of Knowing: The Development of Self, Voice, and Mind* (1986) by Mary Belenky et al. attends to women's experiences and articulating meanings implicit in what women say.[38] Belenky's research study shows the development of the female voice through a variety of stages. She illustrates that women's epistemological development within the context of family and educational systems provides patterns of relationships and communication that affect ways of knowing as much as exposure to information. Belenky argues that theories of human development have been written by men and have focused on male experiences as normative, neglecting or devaluing women's epistemology, with its reliance on personal meaning, self-understanding, and appreciation of the fuller interpersonal context. The studies of Gilligan, Miller, and Belenky provide a necessary critique of the cognitive-structuralist approach's male-dominated research.

Another critique of the cognitive-structuralist approach in general and in faith development theory in particular is the lack of ecclesial diversity represented. In regard to ecclesial affiliation, about 50 percent were Protestant and 35 percent were Roman Catholic or Orthodox. Jewish respondents were overrepresented in the sample, while "other" respondents were underrepresented. The latter category included not only adherents of other traditions such as Muslims, Mormons, and Unitarian Universalists but also those who label themselves "none of the above."[39] A more serious concern about Fowler's sample is its ethnic composition. Only about 2 percent of his interviewees were African American, and he did not even report how many were Hispanic. In contrast, in 2018, 30 percent of the American population was African American (12 percent) and Hispanic (18 percent).[40]

Vanessa Walker and John Snarey have followed Gilligan's thesis by arguing that African Americans come to moral judgments in a unique way. Their ethics of care relates to the influence of the family in moral decision-making. Walker and Snarey argue that the debate between morality influenced by justice, as reflected in Piaget and Kohlberg, and the ethics of care, as reflected by Gilligan, needs to be enlarged by including the voices of African Americans and other minorities.[41]

Also, Rosalie Cohen indicates that black children have a different cognitive style than white children. Cohen argues that children operate from two basic cognitive styles: the analytical style and the relational style. She finds that white children are generally analytical, while black children are generally relational.[42] Black children tend to attribute significance to objects and events only in relationship to specific contexts. Stage theories have defined development as a linear progress in the development of analytic skills and do not consider a person's varying social and cultural contexts when it comes to aspects of growth.[43]

While some of the critiques provided include critiques about the broader structuralist approach, it shows the weakness of the theory by not including as many female voices or persons of color in the study. Also, his theory, which is built on a cognitive-structuralist approach, does not include more on affective dimensions of faith formation.

Conclusion

While Fowler's faith development theory has been critiqued on many fronts, this chapter has argued that Fowler makes a distinction between human faith and Christian faith. Many Christians who have critiqued his theory on the basis of content have misunderstood the difference between human faith and orthodox Christian faith, or as Fowler describes the difference, between faith and belief. While Christians seeking to use Fowler's faith development theory reject his content of faith, they can endorse the structure of his theory. James Loder's theory of convictional knowing, which provides a description of human transformation as the power of convictional knowing in the Spirit, provides Christian religious educators with a credible alternative to Fowler's content and structure of faith development.

Discussion Questions

1. What is James Fowler's definition of *faith*, and how does it differ from an evangelical view of faith?
2. What is the difference between evangelicals' and Fowler's *content* of faith?
3. In what ways does James Loder's view of convictional knowing provide a basis for a Christian view of human transformation?
4. How might faith development be different from the perspective of women and persons of color?
5. How should people educate for faith formation given gender and ethnic diversity?

Further Reading

Astley, Jeff, and Leslie Francis. *Christian Perspective on Faith Development*. Grand Rapids: Eerdmans, 1992.

Chamberlain, Gary L. *Fostering Faith: A Minister's Guide to Faith Development*. New York: Pauline Press, 1988.

Fowler, James W. *Faithful Change: The Personal and Public Challenges of Postmodern Life*. Nashville: Abingdon, 1996.

Jones, Timothy Paul. "The Basis of James W. Fowler's Understanding of Faith in the Research of Wilfred Cantwell Smith: An Examination from an Evangelical Perspective." *Religious Education* 99, no. 4 (2004): 345–57.

Loder, James E. *The Transforming Moment*. Colorado Springs: Helmers & Howard, 1989.

Part 2

Congregational Dimensions of Faith Formation

5

Cultural Challenges to Faith Formation

Our culture seems to be fixated on cakes. Think about it. Channels are full of cake shows: *Fabulous Cakes*, *Cake Boss*, *Ace of Cakes*, *Extreme Cake Makers*, and *Cake Wars*, not to mention the spin-off *Cupcake Wars* as well as all the cake-related shows like *Best Baker* and *The Great British Bake Off*! It is easy to think that all cakes are the same, regardless of their shape. A chocolate cake is chocolate whether in a Bundt mold, a cupcake wrapper, or a rectangular tin. But watch these shows and you will find that this is the wrong assumption. The baking container slightly changes the chemistry and also alters the surface (Bundts produce a crispier surface . . . cupcakes rarely have that). Context is not inert; it is influential.

The context in which our faith is formed has a profound influence on it. How one comes to faith, the types of faith a culture encourages and extols, and the expressions of faith that are not tolerated or affirmed all pose challenges to forming a genuinely Christian faith. This chapter briefly explores the relationship between faith formation and culture and then turns to several challenges to Christian faith formation in Western culture—biblical illiteracy, Moral Therapeutic Deism, and finally the rejection of religious faith among the nones—with attention given to how evangelicals can respond and offer a more substantive alternative to them.

Culture and Faith Formation

The classic work on the relationship between the church and its culture was penned in the mid-twentieth century by Richard Niebuhr. His *Christ and Culture* proposed five relationships between the church and culture that could be demonstrated from the first century forward, existing simultaneously throughout the twenty centuries of church history.[1] Table 5.1 summarizes the relationships proposed by Niebuhr.

If we place these relationships on a spectrum, on one end is faith that is formed by rejecting one's culture, on the other end is faith that is purely

Table 5.1
Niebuhr's Five Approaches to Church and Culture

Relationship	Proponents	Description	Critique
Christ against Culture	1 John Tertullian Tolstoy	Separatistic: radical rejection of any inculturation or contextualization of faith	"A necessary and inadequate position" (Niebuhr) Mission evangelism denied Parallels fundamentalists' anti-intellectualism
Christ of Culture	Gnostics Abelard Kant A. Ritschl	Accommodation: culture is normative and faith is subject to it (i.e., "cultural Protestantism")	Historically, the rise of apocryphal gospels Loss of Christian distinctiveness in culture Cultural elitism, political correctness
Christ above Culture	Justin Martyr Clement of Alexandria Origen Aquinas	Synthesis: affirms the uncritical acceptance of culture and blends it with the Christian faith	A both/and approach An uncritical acceptance of culture Can lead to the affirmation of sin (Niebuhr)
Christ and Culture in Paradox	Paul Martin Luther Maricon	Dualistic: Christians exist within the tension between sources of norms with no definitive direction given to the individual	Can lead to antinomianism (Niebuhr) Can lead to cultural conservatism (Niebuhr) Lacks a holistic perspective
Christ the Transformer of Culture	Gospel of John Augustine F. D. Maurice	Conversion: culture is good as an expression of God's interaction with human history, and hence culture should reflect God's presence (e.g., Augustine's *City of God*)	Can resort to primitivism rather than progressivism No definitive methodology for the transformation process

enculturated, and in the center is faith that is based on Christ as the transformer, who converts culture into a Christian context in which believers can thrive. Culture is not just conducive or condescending toward faith. All cultures have challenges and prospects for faith formation. Faith and its formation are contextualized by culture.

D. A. Carson revisits Niebuhr's classic work in 2008, writing *Christ and Culture Revisited*, wherein he not only critically reassesses Niebuhr's categories but also expresses how believers relate to their culture in an age of postmodernism.[2] He argues that culture is not separate from personal faith but is the context in which it is expressed. He asserts, "We perceive that Christian faith in the New Testament, though doubtless highly personal, was never merely private. Inevitably, the larger culture was going to be confronted— and this included the state" (citing Phil. 2:11; Rev. 11:15; 19:1–9).[3] He later explains that as Christians work out their faith, they do so in the context of the culture in which they live.[4]

Western culture has been on a slope toward secularism for the past several centuries, but it seems to have accelerated its pace in the past few decades. Such a slide toward secularism will indeed pose challenges to the Christian faith and the formation of a distinctively Christian faith, challenges the church and the individual Christian will have to address. In his *Faith Formation in a Secular Age*, Andrew Root describes "secular" in three phases. Secular 1 (sacred versus secular planes) produces the conditions wherein secular 2 (religious versus areligious spaces) can arise, which in turn facilitates the conditions for the advent of secular 3 (the negating of transcendence), wherein the belief in the supernatural is made impossible.[5] In short, we are living in a culture in which religious, and specifically Christian, faith is becoming ancillary, marginalized.

Underscoring this shift toward secularism, Stephen Prothero's *Religious Literacy* underscores the ignorance of most Americans regarding not only the religions of others but also their own faith.[6] Those of us who regard faith as the core of our identity and existence feel like aliens and are perceived as such by the culture in which we live. "Beloved, I urge you as sojourners and exiles to abstain from the passions of the flesh, which wage war against your soul. Keep your conduct among the Gentiles honorable, so that when they speak against you as evildoers, they may see your good deeds and glorify God on the day of visitation" (1 Pet. 2:11–12).

As we will discover throughout this chapter, even in an era of secularization, an affirmation of spirituality remains that values personal spirituality over a personal faith—that is, an institutionalized faith rooted in content. This new notion of "faith," formed in the context of an increasingly secular and postmodern culture, has consequences in regard to Christian faith formation.

In the context of postmodern secularism, faith takes on an intriguing hue. It is a faith that focuses on the individual rather than the object of faith, and it tends to reject logic and reason in favor of subjectivity. Likewise, it rejects the transcultural nature of Christian faith, regarding it as solely Western. This postmodern faith endeavors to construct a consistent approach to life in the absence of a metanarrative for the content of faith.

Faith without Substance: Biblical Illiteracy[7]

What is the Bible? What's in the Bible? What does the Bible mean? How should we use the Bible? Biblical illiteracy takes many forms. Biblical illiteracy can mean ignorance of content or misattribution of the content of Scripture, but both lead to an error in perception of the Bible itself.

While most studies indicate that a majority of Americans hold the Bible in high regard, those same studies indicate that Americans are increasingly ignorant of what is actually in the Bible. As George Gallup and Jim Castelli concluded, "Americans revere the Bible but, by and large, they don't read it. And because they don't read it, they have become a nation of biblical illiterates."[8] Only 50 percent of adults in the United States can provide the title of one Gospel, and most cannot recall the first book of the Bible.[9] The Barna research group has made some other disturbing revelations about Americans' grasp of Bible content and their changing perception of the Bible. Stephen Prothero collected some startling statistics that demonstrate the lack of Bible knowledge among Americans:

- Only half of American adults can even name one of the four Gospels.
- Most Americans cannot name the first book of the Bible.
- Only one-third know that Jesus (not Billy Graham) delivered the Sermon on the Mount.
- A majority of Americans wrongly believe that the Bible says that Jesus was born in Jerusalem.
- One-quarter of Americans think the book of Acts is in the Old Testament. More than one-third say they don't know.
- Most Americans don't know that Jonah is a book in the Bible.
- Ten percent of Americans believe that Joan of Arc was Noah's wife.[10]

George Barna observes that older non-Christians are more biblically literate than younger non-Christians and even believers today.[11] In generations past, even non-Christians had a more significant knowledge of the Bible than their younger counterparts do today. Most Americans are so unfamiliar with the Bible that they fail to recognize or acknowledge biblical references in cultural vernacular, even misattributing them, and they fail to grasp the message and meaning of the Bible even when read, visualized, dramatized, or spoken. Without this familiarity, our culture fails to properly assess the impact Christianity has had, fails to recognize the significant intellectual contribution Christianity has made, and sees Christian faith as ancillary to culture.

A lack of biblical literacy is a challenge not only for American culture but also for the American church, posing a distinctive challenge for faith formation in the twenty-first century. In an interview about his book *Saving the Bible from Ourselves*, Glenn R. Paauw observed that "the Scriptures are meant to play a vital role, and if we don't receive those Scriptures and know them so that their work can be done in our lives, then we're living sub-par Christian lives—not fully flourishing Christian lives."[12] "People are trying to live a Bible-less Christianity."[13] Jason Norris has traced the decline of biblical literacy in the US church.[14] The collapse of biblical literacy within the church is so drastic that it is actually catching up with that of the general US population. "Perhaps surprisingly, born-again and Evangelical teens were often only slightly more likely than other teens to display Bible literacy."[15] In short, biblical illiteracy is a cultural phenomenon that is reflective of the church's own crisis, affecting faith formation for everyone.

Why is biblical illiteracy so prevalent and on the rise now? In our population, there are fewer Christians and hence fewer Bible readers. This, coupled with a loss of the Christian voice in an age of pluralism, and perhaps because the church has moved from Christian formation and discipleship toward a more generic spiritual formation, has marginalized the Bible not only in the culture but also in the church.

Many people experience confusion when trying to study the Bible alone. Due to this confusion and the resulting frustration, readers do not value the Bible as a practical, understandable guide to faith and its formation, they deem the Bible irrelevant to life, and hence they make acquiring biblical knowledge a low priority.

Cultural shifts in the United States have also contributed to the decline in biblical literacy. The advent of postmodernism, with its emphasis on a radically personalized truth and a denial of an external truth, opposing any metanarrative that all must accept as true, certainly contributes to the sense that people do not need to study the Bible to gain relevant spiritual knowledge and insight. In addition, relativism has led many Americans to regard other books as equal to the Bible or the Bible as equal to the others. The Bible's uniqueness has been lost. In addition, lowered expectations for memorization within our culture, which is ever more dependent on access to the written word rather than retention, lends itself to the lack of biblical knowledge.

Evangelism, discipleship, and education are all affected by the loss of biblical literacy, posing a challenge for the twenty-first-century church. The conspicuous absence of the Word of God impairs the potential for faith and its formation. Posing an even greater challenge for churches striving to be relevant to an ever-increasing diverse population, the problem of biblical illiteracy is even more pronounced within minority groups,[16] adding another obstacle to the church's efforts to reach them.

The church faces a devastating twofold dilemma: a simultaneously expanding and shrinking gap between it and the culture. First, the gap between the church and culture is expanding due to society's ever-increasing ignorance of biblical content. Second, unfortunately, the gap is shrinking because the church is also becoming more illiterate about the Bible and significant matters of faith.

A Christian Response to Biblical Illiteracy

The twofold dilemma poses a significant challenge for faith formation in the American church. The American church can no longer assume that Christianity is the norm within the culture, as in previous generations, nor can it assume that professing Christians are significantly more biblically literate than the culture in which they live. What can Christians do?

First, we must embrace the importance of Bible study for ourselves. We do not regard the Bible as just a book or ancient tradition or cultural key but as Scripture. We do not simply want biblical literacy but the outcome of biblical study—that is, faith formation (Matt. 21:42; 22:29; Mark 12:10, 24; John 20:9; Acts 17:11). We do not just want to know the Bible; we want to know God through the Bible. We must not assume that churchgoers will be turned off by a Bible study. We must help both nonbelievers and believers to embrace the Bible as God's Word.

Second, we can no longer assume that people know the story. We can no longer assume that a family owns a Bible, knows where it is, or knows where to turn when we refer to a passage. Evangelists, preachers, and teachers cannot assume that a passing reference to a Bible story is sufficient. It may actually be time to break out the old flannel graph . . . or upgrade to digital video!

Third, we need to introduce the world to biblically based faith formation. We are not the only voices of faith in American culture. Basic tenets of faith formation are often confused or mismatched with elements of non-Christian faiths—for example, meditation in Christianity versus in Eastern religions. Collin Hansen notes that the problem is much greater than people just not knowing the Bible's content. People are endeavoring to live a spiritual life that is more and more biblically ill-informed.[17] Brad Waggoner of the Southern Baptist Convention writes, "To biblically shape the faith to come, spiritual leaders will [need to] do whatever it takes to equip believers in the disciplines of reading, studying, memorizing, and meditating upon God's Word."[18]

Fourth, we need an educational agenda that emphasizes biblical literacy. This is true not only for the church but also for public schools, where the inclusion of biblical or religious literacy is gaining popularity in many states. Such a curriculum includes not just Bible content but also insights into how to use Bible study aids and how to study the Bible for personal growth. Such insights would lower the anxiety and confusion that many experience when trying to study the Scriptures for themselves. Resources and instruction can be provided digitally online in the form of downloads or videos. Resources that enable individuals and groups to engage the biblical text constructively and at their own pace are crucial for raising biblical awareness and facilitating a rise in biblical literacy. As Jason Daye writes, "There's a lot of work in the church to correct not just Bible literacy, but Bible attitudes and expectations for what kind of book this is. If we're going to change the story of the Bible in the church and in the culture, we've got to do more than just pretend like we can give people Bible facts. We've got to give them all the tools to have a great experience and good understanding with the Bible—and then they can have a chance to say 'how does it speak to our life today?'"[19]

Fifth, we need to encourage and facilitate routine Bible reading for faith formation. Glenn R. Paauw, in his book *Saving the Bible from Ourselves*, explains:

> [My] core argument is that for most of us, most of the time, small readings prevail over big readings. "Small" and "big" refer to more than the length of the passages we take in. We define small readings as those diminished samplings of Scripture in which individuals take in fragmentary bits outside of the Bible's literary, historical and dramatic contexts. Also implicated here is a correspondingly meager soteriology—that narrow, individualistic and escapist view of salvation so common among Christians. My hope is that these deficiencies will come to be corrected by big readings. These are the more magnified experiences that result when communities engage natural segments of text, or whole books, taking full account of the Bible's various contexts. This will foster the apprehension of the story's goal in a majestic regeneration that is as wide as God's good creation.[20]

If we are going to get the big picture of the Bible, the full story, we need to read big!

Faith in Who or What? Loss of a Personal God

Faith requires an object; it is not self-existing or self-sustaining. The Christian faith is centered on the person of Jesus Christ. However, the twenty-first-century church finds itself in a culture in which God is a notion, a concept, almost a legitimized figment of our imagination. In *Faith Formation in a Secular Age*, Andrew Root writes about a principle of "subtraction" prevalent in our culture. "The real problem with subtraction stories is that they turn everything, including God, into a concept. Concepts do not necessarily put a demand on me. So if the concept of God helps you be authentically you, then it's worth keeping."[21] What Root is describing is Moralistic Therapeutic Deism (MTD).

The book *Soul Searching*, based on the National Study of Youth and Religion (NSYR) sponsored by the Lily Endowment, was released in 2005. The study concludes that the default religious faith of adolescents in the United States was not the faith expressed in traditional or mainline Christian traditions but rather MTD.[22] MTD has five core beliefs:

1. A God exists who created and orders the world and watches over human life on earth (i.e., deism).

2. God wants people to be good, nice, and fair to one another, as taught in the Bible and by most world religions (i.e., moralistic).

3. The central goal of life is to be happy and to feel good about oneself (i.e., therapeutic).

4. God does not need to be particularly involved in one's life except when God is needed to resolve a problem (i.e., deism and therapeutic).

5. Good people go to heaven when they die (i.e., moralistic and therapeutic).[23]

A follow-up study to *Soul Searching* was conducted by Christian Smith with Patricia Snell. They conclude that MTD remained prevalent even into early adulthood.[24] However, as people transitioned from adolescence into emerging adulthood, facing more adult life challenges and problems, in many instances their MTD waned or was rejected as being unrealistic and insufficient.[25] In adulthood, those maintaining their MTD seemed to fall into predictable patterns, with a faith formation rooted in personal authority, a cafeteria approach to religious beliefs, a self-vindicating "blind faith," and an emphasis on personal choice.[26]

Among young people, MTD continues to be the preferred alternative to faith and faith formation as typically described in a Christian context, posing a cultural challenge to the church and its disciple-making mission of bringing people to faith. Kendra Creasy Dean comments, "Line up the Apostles' Creed beside the assumptions of Moralistic Therapeutic Deism sometime: They bear little resemblance to one another in either tone or substance. The Apostles' Creed is a dramatic, sweeping description of God's wildest ideas . . . while Moralistic Therapeutic Deism sounds like the Declaration of Independence in Sunday School."[27]

A Christian Response to Moral Therapeutic Deism

Andrew Root cautions that the way to overcome MTD is not just a new process—that is, new curriculums and approaches to faith formation itself. It is not that simple.[28] The simple fact is that many adolescents and young adults have opted for MTD because of the ways in which the church endeavored to demonstrate relevance and to reiterate propositional truth through indoctrination. These methods alienated adolescents and young people a generation ago.[29] As Nels Ferré warned Christian educators in 1954, "The direct learning of social, moral, and spiritual wisdom is seldom applied by the learner because it has not been personally appropriated. Education suffers from a chronic indigestion of unassimilated propositional truths."[30] What is needed is a new approach to appropriating the Christian faith and fostering its formation, one that engages critical thinking within the context of faith to cause self-examination and a turning to the faith to find answers. Critical thinking about faith demonstrates the futility of MTD, moves people toward openness to the Christian faith, and provides the practices that will continue their faith formation.

Jesus was often critical of noncritical thinkers, especially when noncritical thinking led to blind obedience to religious leaders.[31] This is often depicted in Matthew's Gospel (12:12–14; 15:1–7; 19:1–28). Jesus's way of responding to a question with a question was not a way of avoiding the question but of facilitating critical thinking in the questioner's mind as a means of faith formation. When Jesus was in conflict with religious authorities, such as the Pharisees, Sadducees, and Jerusalem officials, he used critical thinking to challenge their assumptions and conclusions. Hence, Jack Dean Kingsbury describes Jesus as provoking, triggering, or inciting conflict with the religious authorities so as to create a more conducive learning environment.[32] Jesus challenged their assumptions (e.g., Sadducees' understanding of resurrection and marriage; Matt. 22:23–33; Mark 12:18–27; Luke 20:27–40), their allegations (e.g., Beelzebub; Matt. 12:22–27; Mark 3:20–30), and their hypocrisy (e.g., healing on the Sabbath; Matt. 9:1–8; Mark 2:1–12; Luke 5:17–26). He

forced them to critique themselves before critiquing him, which is essential
to critical thinking and faith formation.

Larry Richards observes that many evangelical Christians believe that since
the Bible is God's Word, authoritative or transmissive approaches to teaching
it are all that are required.[33] However, he disagrees with this conclusion. Methods beyond indoctrination must be used, including those that engage critical
thinking. Faith must become "habitual"—for example, the recitation of the
Lord's Prayer or the Apostles' Creed is a habit—but it must move beyond a
habit in order to transform life.[34] Michael Warren speaks of a congregation as
a comprehensive context of critical thinking that provides permission for the
"free discussion of complex issues." In the absence of such an environment,
"the role of the laity is to be consumers of the religious insights of others.
They are invited to reproduce religious speech, instead of engaging in the
original coproduction of religious insight."[35] Eugene Roehlkepartain raises
the following questions in this regard:

- Are questions encouraged or discouraged?
- How does the congregation deal with diverse opinions?
- Are members challenged to examine their faith and everyday lives?
- How do leaders model a thinking faith?
- Are youth given answers, or are they led to discover answers?[36]

Failure to engage critical thinking keeps the Christian faith at arm's length,
something we rent rather than own—the perfect seedbed for MTD. If we
want to pass faith to the next generation, it has to be more than an inherited
heirloom. It has to be something to which they add their distinctive mark. If
the church becomes an institution in which critical thinking is not welcomed
or facilitated, youth will simply find another outlet for their thoughts, feelings,
and faith. But if the church can become a place of critical thinking within an
atmosphere of faith, then it can be a seedbed for thoughts, feelings, and faith.

Spirituality without Faith: "The Nones"[37]

We have all taken the surveys and censuses that routinely circulate, color-
ing in little boxes or dots to reply to personal questions. One typical item is
religious affiliation. Following the list of the major religious identities (e.g.,
Christian, Muslim, Jew, Buddhist, Hindu) and sometimes even specific deri-
vations of those religions (e.g., Catholic, Protestant, evangelical) is the box
typically located at the end labeled "none." These are the people who identify

themselves as having no religious affiliation, no religious identity, no discernable faith tradition. The nones.

The subject of the nones in US culture actually goes back to the groundbreaking work in 1968 of sociologist Glenn M. Vernon, who notes "that the religious 'none' or independent is a phenomenon worthy of study."[38] However, what began as a curious cultural anomaly is now descriptive of almost an entire generation. From 1970 to 1990, nones were a steady 7 percent of the US population, but they rose to 17 percent in 2010. Among eighteen to twenty-nine year olds, nones rose from 12 to 27 percent between 1990 and 2010.[39] Because they are nones, their religious identity is at best nebulous. They are not a homogeneous group, and often false assumptions are made about them, leading to poor endeavors by the church to reach them . . . which may in fact only bolster their none-ness.

Describing the Landscape

Not all nones are alike. They cannot be lumped into one large category with broadly articulated descriptors. They are in fact a very heterogeneous group. John Condran and Joseph Tamney studied nones from 1957 to 1982, echoing similar studies done in 1970 and 1980, to both describe and explain why people self-identify as none.[40] They suggest two kinds of nones based on their research.

- *Structural nones* are those who are isolated from religious institutions or "workers" who reject religion because of its favor of management. They do not like organizations like the church or organized religion.
- *Cultural nones* do not affirm the characteristics of religious organizations; that is, they reject "their outreach and social alignments," their social morals and imposition of standards on culture, and the church's politicization.[41]

More recent attempts have been made to categorize or analyze the none population. The most common categorization has a threefold division: atheist, agnostic, and religious[42] (or atheist, agnostic, and unchurched believer).[43]

A further dimension to the none population involves their view toward religion.

- *Religious nones* do not identify with a particular religious preference, but some tend to weave in and out of religious identity and preference.[44] Some maintain some religious beliefs, such as a belief in God, a supreme being, or a force, and some engage in religious practices, such as prayer, yoga, meditation, and even church attendance.[45]

- *Secular nones* espouse no religious beliefs or practices.

The religious nones can be further divided into liminal and stable.[46]

- *Liminal nones* are those who are half in and half out of religious identity, occupying the space "between faith and doubt."[47]
- *Stable nones* are those who are either in or out of religious identity.

According to Chaeyoon Lim, there are more liminal nones than stable nones.[48]

While many suggest that nones are simply spiritual seekers, no real recent evidence proves that nones are seekers or that they merely favor religious individualism. And of course, such a view doesn't even apply to a secular none.[49] Drew Dyck notes that while nones are not necessarily atheists, they often have a sense of spiritual delusion, many times "for a host of unbiblical reasons"—for example, family members were hyper-fundamentalist, which led to a desensitivity toward a more formal or organized faith.[50] Some nones have "less confidence in the clergy,"[51] or they are not amenable to organized religion because they affirm that spirituality and faith are personal and private and do not belong in the public sphere or the political arena.[52] For example, when Donald Trump was elected president, actor Alec Baldwin cryptically tweeted, "One thing that is changed forever in this country is the meaning of the word 'Christian' as it applies to politics."[53] This kind of sentiment is typical among nones.

Some nones are "spiritual," just not religious or affirming of faith in the traditional sense. Elizabeth Drescher comments that nones have "fluid spiritual communities" and "interwoven stories of the self," and they do not represent "a turn away from religion, but rather the emergence of multiple, sometimes overlapping, sometimes diverging narratives of religious and spiritual experiences."[54] While this may sound confusing and even contradictory, the reason is simple. For members of the Christian faith, what would be described as an organized religion, the ideas of spirituality, faith, and religion are not synonymous, but they are considered intricately related, virtually inseparable. However, for nones, the notions of spirituality, faith, and religion are separate matters, distinct from one another and not interdependent.[55] Faith is considered a lifestyle, a premodern worldview, the content of belief. It is accepted as binding universal truth without requiring any evidence. Religion is institutional, organizational, concrete, and ritualistic, the product of a very modern worldview. But spirituality is mysterious, nebulous, a union of

Figure 5.1

Atheist	Agnostic	Religious
Nones	Nones	Nones

Antagonistic	Favorable
toward Religion	toward Religion

faith and religion that is more embracing and inclusive than they are, with its contemporary expression being fueled by a postmodern worldview. This is why nones can seem genuine, honest, and sincere when discussing spiritual matters. Their beliefs are *their* beliefs, with no middlemen or institution to mediate their beliefs for them.[56]

So how do nones really view religion? Figure 5.1 illustrates a spectrum ranging from "antagonistic toward religion" to "favorable toward religion." Nones most often fill the left side of the spectrum. Atheist nones are the most antagonistic toward religion, with agnostic nones being not as against religion. Religious nones generally occupy the center of the spectrum, still being nones without necessarily being antagonistic toward religion. Why are they not on the right side? Because their nonantagonistic posture toward religion is evident, but if they traveled any further right on the spectrum, they would cease to be nones. For example, one study showed that liminal religious nones more frequently marry non-nones and even desire for their children to adopt a religious affiliation, which means that the next generation doesn't share in the secularization process.[57]

Where Did Their Faith Go? Why Are They Nones?

So why are people nones? Perhaps one of the most insightful recent works on the subject is *The Rise of the Nones* by James Emery White. He describes the two "perfect storms" that formed a cultural context that was conducive for the rise of the none population.

- First perfect storm: This involved the marginalizing of religion (and God) as a means of rationalizing and understanding the universe—that is, the implications of the research of Copernicus (Earth is no longer the universe's center), Darwin (human origins have an alternative answer to creation), and Freud (the human psyche can be understood by its component parts). God was slowly marginalized from cosmology, biology, and psychology.
- Second perfect storm: This involved the association of religion (and God) with cultural elements that are objectionable to nones—that is,

political engagement by organized religion, God's name being connected to irreligious ideas like guns, the use of religion to accumulate vast wealth, and the scandals and materialism of religious leaders.[58]

These storms provided the canvas for a spirituality without faith, making it increasingly difficult for the church to reach nones. So what can the church do?

A Christian Response to the Nones

Perhaps the most substantial obstacle to overcome in discipling nones is "Christian privilege."[59] Many believers and church leaders in congregations of all theological stripes approach their communities and culture as if Christendom were still present—that is, a physical domain in which Christian belief informs the culture and the church is a dominant authority, such as in medieval Europe. Approaching the none population with this assumption is simply repulsive to them and futile for the church. If we think we are the only spiritual voice in our culture, the Bible is the only religious text, Christ is the only recognized Savior, and the God of the Bible is the only view of deity, we obviously don't exegete contemporary music, literature, movies, television, or websites. The church and the culture, especially the none population within the culture, are currently on two different frequencies, two different channels, two different settings . . . and hence no one is listening to the other.

What the church needs is an approach to engaging the none population in a more constructive and conducive manner. The following suggestions offer ways for the church to more intentionally reach the none population with the gospel.

Provide liminal space. The church needs to provide a "space in between" for nones. Traditional approaches to discipleship advocate a sequential, unilateral pattern of believe–belong–behave. However, nones seem to be more attracted to belong–believe–behave. They want to try something out, take a spiritual test drive, prior to making a commitment. This means that the church has to make room for individuals who want to participate in the church before affirming their faith or behaving like believers. How many churches say you have to be a Christian even to play on the softball team? No, nones cannot be teachers, leaders, or pastors in the church, but there have to be some areas where they can engage in Christian service alongside believers, places where they can openly explore the mystery of the Christian faith.[60] To the previously identified three-step pattern should be added one more: become![61] An approach to discipling nones must provide space to explore doubt. Popular books like David Kinnaman's *You Lost Me* and *UnChristian* by David Kinnaman and Gabe Lyons express the need for the church to become more sensitive toward doubt rather than posturing itself as the exclusive and exhaustive purveyor of all knowledge.

Use opportune moments. In 1979, C. Kirk Hadaway and Wade Clark Roof demonstrated that many nones shifted toward affirming a religious identity or affiliating with a specific faith when they physically moved to a new location. Regardless of the nature of the move, the change in context seemed to make some nones more open to meeting others through church and other religious activities.[62] Since 1979, new social, quasi-religious options have arisen, such as the Sunday Assembly, aka Atheist Church in England.[63] Other such nonreligious routine gatherings have also arisen in the United States. But the principle still remains that nones are more open to new experiences, even religious ones, when they relocate or experience a life-altering event. Such events facilitate introspection and reassessment of one's situation, and hence religion is given an opportunity to speak into their lives.

Stress relationships. Evangelism and discipleship are predicated on relationship. In almost every instance, regardless of the circumstance, having a prior relationship with an individual is a crucial factor, but more so with nones. Relationship is essential to successful disciple making with them. College chaplain Teri McDowell Ott comments, "Sometimes my conversations with the nones feel more honest, more real," primarily because, "when talking to the nones, I can't use religion as a fallback position." In such conversations, relationship replaces religion as the basis for the discussion.[64] Essentially, one must earn the right to share Christ with a none by establishing a genuine one-on-one relationship before interjecting religion into it.

Use new teaching formats. Religious instruction, the content of faith, and the traditions of religion cannot be forced on nones. However, "if religion becomes a choice rather than something handed down . . . [religious communities or church] will also become communities of choice rather than default ones based on a semblance of belief."[65] This realization requires Christian educators to develop a new approach to teaching (rather than the proverbial speaking to the choir) if they are to connect with a population that has an entirely different set of receptors to religious instruction.

Most universities have an introduction to religion course, but teaching it as an introduction to Christianity course is problematic to nones. Caryn D. Riswold formulates several teaching tactics for instructing nones that do not lean on the tendency of Christian privilege.[66] Her tactics include the following:

1. Use questions, not statements, to study the content of faith, enabling the student to explore and form an answer within the faith context without a preconceived response to matters of faith.

2. Introduce definitions that are more about how and why than what. In this way, the teacher focuses students on the process and importance of determining a definition rather than simply a predetermined dictionary response.

3. Focus on topics that facilitate conversation between Christianity and other religions (even atheism) among students so that the distinctiveness and depth of a Christian answer can be affirmed.

4. Utilize multiple sacred texts. Introduce students to texts of other religions, providing access to primary sources rather than just talking about them in the third person, and allow students to draw their own conclusions about their teaching.

These tactics may seem to undermine instruction in the Christian faith and even undermine faith formation, but in fact these measures enable students, Christian or none, to form a personal affirmation of faith rather than just inheriting the faith of others. For the none, these methods place Christian faith on an equal plane with other world religions and facilitate their own independent exploration into it in relation to other faith traditions, enabling them to accept it somewhat on their own terms.

Be open about your faith. We are backing off from proclamation, creating a safe space as the none population approaches the church. This is not altogether appropriate. But we do want to present the Christian faith in such a way that nones can more readily hear, consider, and of course eventually affirm it than is the case with many traditional efforts.

Drew Dyck recommends what he describes as a Luke 14:26–27 approach to discipling nones.[67] Luke 14:26–27 says, "If anyone comes to me and does not hate his own father and mother and wife and children and brothers and sisters, yes, and even his own life, he cannot be my disciple. Whoever does not bear his own cross and come after me cannot be my disciple." What does this have to do with nones? How does this passage make you feel about the Christian faith? About being a disciple? Dyck affirms that it is acceptable to make nones uncomfortable, to make them face the gospel, to push them off their nominal, generic, lukewarm position and even force engagement. He suggests that perhaps nones are nones because of the church's nominal attention to the gospel and all its implications. "My prayer for the church is that we will cease perpetuating this great scandal. When faced with the all-or-nothing demands of the gospel, many nominal Christians will respond with genuine faith. Others will walk away."[68]

Nones represent a growing segment of the population, one that the traditional approaches to evangelism and discipleship seem to fail. If the church is going to reach and teach the none segment of our communities, we must first understand the intricacies of the group and form a distinctive approach to engage them with the gospel. Faith formation isn't just for those already in the church or already in the faith. It must extend to those with no religious affiliation, the nones. Reaching them requires a unique approach to evangelism.

Conclusion

The culture in which the Christian faith now grows is quite distinct from that of a hundred, fifty, or even twenty-five years ago. Each era presents unique challenges to the formation of faith. However, it likewise offers opportunities for the church to rise up and meet those challenges, passing on the faith to the next generation, becoming more resilient than the last. The proverbial statement "What doesn't kill you only makes you stronger" certainly applies to faith formation, as it has over the past centuries and even today.

Discussion Questions

1. On the spectrum created by Richard Niebuhr, where do you find yourself? Why there?
2. In what ways can you promote biblical literacy for yourself and for those to whom you minister?
3. Moralistic Therapeutic Deism affects everyone to some degree. When you read about it, did you find yourself "looking in a mirror"? To what degree? How can you address this in your own faith formation?
4. How do you present faith to those who profess none?

Further Reading

Carson, D. A. *Christ and Culture Revisited*. Grand Rapids: Eerdmans, 2008.

Cox, Harvey. *The Future of Faith*. San Francisco: HarperOne, 2009.

Paauw, Glenn R. *Saving the Bible from Ourselves*. Downers Grove, IL: InterVarsity, 2016.

Root, Andrew. *Faith Formation in a Secular Age*. Grand Rapids: Baker Academic, 2017.

Smith, Christian, with Patricia Snell. *Souls in Transition*. New York: Oxford University Press, 2009.

White, James Emery. *The Rise of the Nones*. Grand Rapids: Baker Books, 2014.

6

Faith Formation
in Community

As described in chapter 5, a growing number of people are becoming
less affiliated with the church, particularly when it comes to their
faith formation. The rise of the nones has resulted in a decline in
church attendance and consistent participation in congregational life. These
trends are discouraging, especially since faith formation is most deeply affected by participation and relationship in a faith community.

Throughout Scripture, the Israelites and the church were formed and shaped
into the people of God through their participation in communal rituals and
practices. Whether it was the Israelites following the teachings of the Torah
and worshiping in the synagogues or the newly formed Christian community
gathered to fellowship and break bread together, the role of the faith community was essential to their faith formation. Since human beings are social
creatures, it is natural that community is formative for a life of faith. As theologian John Wesley states, "The gospel of Christ knows of no religion but
social; no holiness but social holiness."[1]

Wesley's social religion wasn't focused on aspects of social justice but on
human relationships. Wesley knew deeply that growing in God's grace required
being with other Christians on the journey of faith. When one thinks about their
faith journey, they recognize the impact their particular faith community has
in nurturing their faith as they participate in the life of that community. Faith
communities and their practices are critical components of faith formation.

The Community of Faith

Christian educators have given particular focus to the role that faith in community plays in faith formation. Some of these influential theorists include Horace Bushnell, George Albert Coe, C. Ellis Nelson, John Westerhoff III, and Lawrence Richards. This section explores the literature on how faith formation theory has been expressed in Christian religious education, including Christian nurture, social learning theory, and catechesis.

Christian Nurture

One of the most influential and controversial theorists is Horace Bushnell. In his book *Christian Nurture*, published in 1861, he argues that the main focus of Christian education should be "that a child . . . grow up a Christian."[2] He argues that instead of raising a child to be converted at a later date, which was the practice and theory prevalent in the revivalist movement, Christian parents should raise their children from their earliest days to love God and to follow after his ways.[3] His view of Christian nurture assumes that the seed of right principle will be planted by the family and the church and when rightfully cultivated will bring forth a true faith. For Bushnell, Christianization involves not so much a dramatic decision but a process of formation.[4]

Bushnell believes that a distinction of humanity is the ability to pass on to the next generation its gifts, principles, and virtues—so why not by the same process pass on its Christian faith? For Bushnell, the primary medium of passing on the Christian faith is Christian parents. To Bushnell, to live a distinctly Christian life is to nurture.[5] He states, "How different the kind of life that is necessary to bring them up in conversion and beget them anew in the spirit of loving obedience to God, at a point even prior to all definite recollection. This is Christian nurture, because it nurtures Christians and because it makes an element of Christian grace in the house. It invites, it nourishes hope, it breathes in love, it forms the new life as a holy, though beautiful prejudice in the soul, before its opening the full flowering of intelligence arrives."[6]

He believes that children of believing parents should be treated differently than children of unbelievers. Children should be baptized as infants and then regarded as having the basic elements of their parents' faith in them. It is at this point that critics attack him because they think he does not believe in original sin and that he rejects the need for repentance and conversion.[7] Bushnell argues for his view of "organic connection" by stating the following: "Once more, if we narrowly examine the relationship of the parent and child we shall not fail to discover something like a law of organic connection, as regards character, subsisting between them. Such a connection as makes it easy to believe, and natural to expect that the faith of one will be propagated in the other. Perhaps I should rather say, such a connection as induced the conviction that the character of one is actually included in that of the other as a seed is formed in the capsule."[8]

Bushnell argues that just as natural characteristics are hereditary and are passed on to children, faith is also hereditary. He believes that the home and parental influences are of primary importance in the faith development of children. This organic connection is the heart of Christian nurture.

Social Learning Theory

While Bushnell's theory met with stark criticism, it influenced the next generation of social theorists and their understanding of the role that the faith community plays in shaping faith. George Albert Coe argues in his acclaimed book *A Social Theory of Religious Education* (1917) that "the constant aim of elementary religious education should be to make conversion unnecessary."[9] Coe argues that social interaction is the heart of Christian education not only as process but also as content. He holds to the idea of "creative" rather than "transmission" education. Creative education places primary emphasis on social reconstruction and employs transmissive practices only to that end. Coe asserts that the historic aim of individual salvation must be replaced by the broader, more inclusive aim of reconstruction and that transmissive practices must be abandoned in favor of vital participation in social interaction.[10]

The influence of Bushnell and Coe was reflected in the field of Christian religious education, as it shifted from a focus on personal conversion to social reconstruction as the primary means of faith formation. While Bushnell's and Coe's views can be critiqued on many levels, particularly in regard to the role of personal conversion, their theories influenced the next generation of theorists such as C. Ellis Nelson and John Westerhoff III.

In his landmark book, *Where Faith Begins*, Nelson indicates that religion is located within a person's sentiment and is the result of the way they were socialized by the adults who cared for them as a child. Therefore, the "natural agency" for communicating Christian faith is a Christian community. Faith is communicated as persons of faith interact with others. Nelson writes, "Faith is communicated by a community of believers and the meaning of faith is developed by its members out of their history, by their interaction with each other, and in relation to the events that take place in their lives."[11] He continues, "Faith can only be nurtured within a self-conscious intentional community of faith."[12] For Nelson, it is important to identify the ways in which this socialization process can be made more intentional and thus more effective.[13] He particularly focuses on observation and imitation as central to formation. As Perry Downs states, Nelson is "the first of the current religious educators to build his theory solidly on a socialization model" and to tie this to the roles of observation and imitation in religious education theory.[14]

Catechesis

John Westerhoff III views catechesis as a pastoral activity through which faith is nurtured. Westerhoff's thesis of catechesis is best expressed in the book *A Faithful Church: Issues in the History of Catechesis*.[15] According to Westerhoff, catechesis, which is intentional learning within a community of Christian faith and life, is the process by which Christians are made. After baptism, Christians spend the rest of their lives involved in a process of becoming more Christian. This lifelong process is one of catechesis. Catechesis and Christian education are not synonymous. Catechesis is essentially a pastoral activity intended to transmit the church's tradition and to enable faith to become living, conscious, and active in the lives of maturing persons and in the life of a maturing community.[16] It is concerned not only with conversion and nurture, commitment and behavior, but also with aiding the community to become more Christian. It is about passing on living tradition in the form of a story and a vision and is for all those who share in the life and mission of the Christian faith community.[17]

Westerhoff affirms, "Catechesis is the deliberate (intentional), systematic (related) and sustained (life-long) process within a community of Christian faith and life which establish, build up, equip, and enable it to be Christ's body or presence in the world to the end that all people are restored to unity with God and each other."[18] He provides three aspects of catechesis: formation, education, and instruction. *Formation* implies "shaping" and refers to intentional, relational, experiential activities within the life of a story-formed faith community. *Education* implies "reshaping" and refers to critical, reflective activities related to these communal experiences. And *instruction* implies "building" and refers to the means by which knowledge and skills useful to communal life are transmitted, acquired, and understood through a teaching process. Formation forms the body of Christ, education reforms it, and instruction builds it up. According to Westerhoff, these three distinct processes are interrelated in catechesis: "Catechesis is more a process of nurture and conversion than of education though it is concerned for deliberate, systematic, and sustained efforts. Catechesis is a process that is without apology value laden, a process which aims to introduce persons into a community of Christian faith with its distinctive values, understandings, and ways, a process which aims to aid persons to internalize and adopt the community's faith as their own and to apply that faith to life in the world."[19]

A primary function of catechesis is to help the faithful individually and corporately meet the twofold responsibilities that faith asks of them: communion with God and communion with one's fellow human beings—that is, to nurture the intimacy of the spiritual life that expresses itself in social justice, liberation, and the political struggle for whole community, peace, and the well-being of all persons.

Westerhoff's focus on the hidden curriculum as compared to the school-instruction paradigm places him in the enculturation theorist camp as well. According to Westerhoff, the school-instructional paradigm has dominated contemporary thinking. Any attempt to "de-school" society or question the adequacy of instruction is either ignored or met with hostility. For Westerhoff, the school-instructional paradigm is inadequate because it eliminates the process of religious socialization from the concern and attention of church educators and parishioners. "By socialization he means all formal and informal influences through which persons acquire their understandings and ways of living."[20] No one intentionally sits down and teaches life principles; they are learned without school or instruction. Therefore, the informal, hidden curriculum of churches is often more influential in forming faith than the formal curriculum of church schools. As a result, Westerhoff proposes a paradigm of enculturation in the faith community involving all of life.[21]

Westerhoff recognizes the strong enculturation provided by a child's parents and faith community. Individual interaction with people in the faith community provides the "natural agency" for communicating Christian faith. Liturgy and worship are a vital avenue for this communication. Westerhoff says that "the fundamental issue for Christian nurture is ecclesiology, the nature of the church or Christian community."[22] The faith community has a "narrative character." The liturgy and rituals are rich, the memories are handed down to generations, and the "common vision" connects the present to the past and will connect the present to the future. "Worship is the heart of the faith community and is its authority. Christian nurture is dependent upon experience and reflection with the faith community."[23]

To facilitate socialization, there must be catechesis in the church because it assumes a communal understanding of human nature and the necessity of a faithful community, a community that shares a common memory and vision, is conscious of its roots, and is committed to the vision of the future.[24]

In his book *A New Face for the Church*, Lawrence O. Richards views Christian education as one aspect of the faith community, and he sees the entire educational environment as a means of faith formation. He believes that if the church functions effectively, as described in the New Testament, then it will be a nurturing environment that will produce vivacious Christlikeness.[25] He roots his view of the socialization of faith more in a theological perspective than in a sociological perspective. Like Nelson and Westerhoff, Richards believes that faith as life is best transferred by the more relational socialization model than by the Sunday school or instructive classroom model. He believes that faith is learned more like culture and is best passed on through relationships and modeling, through worship, fellowship, and small groups.

Faith Formation in the Community of Faith

Faith formation involves all aspects of a faith community's life. It is primarily affected by how the practices of the community shape, form, and transform people. The role of the church is to create communities of faith that serve God and love neighbors for the sake of transforming the world. Faith formation in the community of faith takes place through the corporate educational effort that nurtures and forms faith within the church and where the witness of the community occurs in the world.[26]

All of the intentional activities within the faith community, including worship, education, service, and mission in the world, are essential aspects of faith formation. Such formation involves not only understanding the primary purposes of congregations but also engaging in specific formative processes that regularly shape Christian life. Jack Seymour maps four prominent approaches to congregational learning:

1. *Social transformation.* Assisting people to promote faithful citizenship and social transformation. The goal is to help Christians see an alternative way of being in the world.

2. *Faith formation.* Fostering authentic relationships to help people engage in community. The goal is to help people engage in community and the outer world.

3. *Spiritual formation.* Helping Christians develop their inner lives and respond with outer action in the world. The goal is to connect Christians to the deep resources of Christian faith and call them to relationship, friendship, justice, and care.

4. *Religious instruction.* Providing learning grounded in the biblical faith that helps people make connections between the content and living out their faith. The goal is to prepare people with the story of Scripture in order for them to live responsibly in the world.[27]

All of these aspects are central to a congregation's process of shaping and forming faith. Every congregation is different and reflects a particular faith tradition and narrative. Whether the congregation is connected to a formal denomination or not, the transmission of the gospel story is reflected in the ways in which the people of God engage in congregational practices. Individuals and congregations have a corporate memory that has been shaped by rituals, theological traditions, stories, and narratives that have been passed on to them. Congregational memory includes the recognition of one's place in the faith tradition and how that tradition will be carried to the next generation. Charles Foster expresses concern that congregations continue to lose corporate memory, especially with the loss of connectedness across generations and diminishing loyalty to particular faith traditions.[28] For those who have participated in a faith community, this sense of corporate memory is very strong, but for many who are new to the church, there is no corporate memory. One of the primary tasks of faith communities is to pass on the faith through their practices to those who do not have a corporate memory.

Fundamentally, humans are created for relationship with God, with others, and with creation, and God is the one who accompanies the search for authentic relationship. It is through a community of grace that relationships with God and one another are nurtured. The church's ministry of forming

Figure 6.1
Congregational Formation

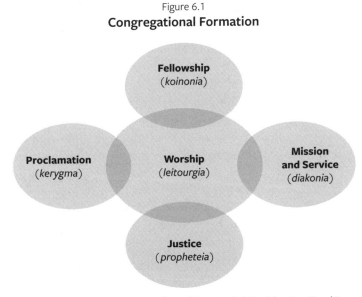

Adapted from Robert W. Pazmiño, *Foundational Issues in Christian Education* (Grand Rapids: Baker, 1997), 45.

faith is about helping others hear God's invitation to relationship and then respond to God's grace through faithful discipleship.[29] Congregations draw on the Christian tradition to shape people's responses through participation in the rituals of faith.

Since all of congregational life fosters faith formation, it is impossible to identify all the significant practices. However, some foundational practices that foster faith formation, based on Robert Pazmiño's book *Foundational Issues in Christian Education*, include worship (*leitourgia*), fellowship (*koinonia*), preaching (*kerygma*), mission and service (*diakonia*), and justice (*propheteia*) (see fig. 6.1).[30]

Worship (Leitourgia)

Worship literally means "ascribing worth to someone." *Leitourgia* means "the work of the people" (*egan*, "work"; *laos*, "people"). The gathering of Christians for worship includes praise and thanksgiving, Scripture reading, proclamation of the gospel, prayer, sharing in Communion, and a charge to live out a life of faith.[31] The primary purpose of Christian communal worship is the glorification of God and the sanctification of humanity. It is a divine-human event in which God offers transformation and healing to help people become more fully what God created them to be. God gathers together individual Christians to heal, transform, and renew them as the body of Christ to send them out to continue the ministry of the incarnation as they participate in the kingdom of God coming more fully. One day the consummation of the kingdom will come, and God will be all in all.[32]

Debra Dean Murphy believes that worship is central to faith formation. She states, "All efforts at forming and discipling Christians should presume the centrality of worship. Through worship, praise, and doxology Christians are formed and transformed."[33] Like Westerhoff, Murphy believes that a more robust ecclesiology instead of a social science approach is needed for faith formation, and it begins with worship. Faith communities are the "natural agency" for communicating the Christian faith, and liturgy and worship are vital avenues for this communication. As Westerhoff says, "The fundamental issue for Christian nurture is ecclesiology, the nature of the Church or Christian community."[34] Worship is the heart of the faith community and is its authority, and thus it is essential in defining the meaning of the church. Catechesis in the church assumes a communal understanding of human nature and the necessity of a faithful community. A community shares a common memory and vision; it is conscious of its roots and committed to the vision of the future.[35] Catechesis is a journey of transformation that culminates in the praise and adoration of God. It begins and ends with liturgy, giving praise and worship to God. Thus, worship confers and nurtures Christian identity.

Each worship practice plays a role in nurturing this identity. Throughout the history of the church, the center of worship has been the proclamation of the gospel (Word) and participation in Communion (Table). Communion is a means of spiritual growth because it heals, preserves, and sustains Christians. It is a "means of grace" in which congregants can encounter God. While many Protestant congregations focus on the Word on a weekly basis, many do not practice Communion weekly. These Protestant congregations give more focus to Scripture as central to formation as reflected in the Protestant Reformation. Many congregations view themselves as low churches with less formal liturgies, lectionary readings, and sacramental theology. However, a sacramental renewal is taking place in many congregations that are practicing Communion weekly.

Most Protestant denominations have two sacraments: Communion and baptism. Baptism marks the entrance into the faith community. A person is baptized into the faith community as an infant or as an adult who accepts Christ. While different faith traditions place an emphasis on either infant baptism or adult baptism, both are important as a sacrament in which grace is received and the recipient becomes a member of the faith community. Through baptism, by the work of the Holy Spirit, a person dies to sin and is resurrected to new life in Jesus Christ. Baptism is a formative practice that provides meaning and identity to members of the faith community.

Charles Foster identifies other significant events that are part of the worshiping life of a church and provide faith formation.

Paradigmatic events establish a pattern of Christian life and community and have their origins in ancient traditions and rituals. They include the reading of the creeds or confessions from a particular faith tradition.

Seasonal events are rhythmical patterns of congregational formation that include the Christian calendar. The Christian calendar provides a basic structure for worship and can include lectionary readings. Lectionary readings are Bible passages used for reading, studying, or preaching that come from the Old Testament, Psalms, Gospels, and Epistles.

Occasional events intensify community identity and mission by providing meaning and shared history. These events include weddings, funerals, anniversaries, mission trips, homecomings, and church building dedications.[36]

Unexpected events interrupt the rhythmic patterns and structures that give order to the worshiping community. These unexpected events bring joy and sorrow. A tragic loss of life, the loss of employment, the birth of a child with a disease, and natural disasters are examples of unexpected events that interrupt the normal flow of congregational life and worship.[37]

Each of these events shapes and forms the faith of the people of God as they worship and live life together. Worship is formative as people gather to praise, hear Scripture read and preached, and participate in the telling and retelling of the story of the gospel.

Fellowship (Koinonia)

Acts 2:42 reports that the new converts to Christianity "devoted themselves to the apostles' teaching and the fellowship, to the breaking of bread and the prayers." The word for fellowship is *koinonia*. *Koinonia* means "communion" or "joint participation." In the New Testament, the word appears in contexts where the collective well-being of the community supersedes the self-interest of the individual members. In other words, everyone is to work and produce for the sake of the community. The early Christians met together in homes to learn about the apostles' teachings, to receive support and encouragement through fellowship, and to spend time in prayer for one another. These early Christians understood the importance of relationship as they struggled with the challenges of life. Christians today are also to be present with one another for times of prayer, confession, and fellowship. *Koinonia* takes place in and through a variety of social events in faith communities, including Sunday school classes, small groups, potlucks, and community events. Christians find small groups meaningful because they provide a means for developing community and relationships with other Christians. They are a place where people can build bonds of friendship and accountability. *Koinonia* is often difficult in a Western individualistic culture, but faith formation takes place as people are willing to share life together.

Preaching (Kerygma)

Kerygma means "proclamation." It finds its origin in the ancient world, where a king would send his heralder to go forth and proclaim the king's decrees. Jesus did something similar at the beginning of his ministry, proclaiming, "The time is fulfilled, and the kingdom of God is at hand; repent and believe in the gospel" (Mark 1:15). Jesus announced the coming of the kingdom and invited people to participate in that new kingdom. *Kerygma* is used in several New Testament passages, such as Jesus's call to proclamation in Luke 4:18–19. Romans 10:14 says that those who proclaim the good news are necessary so that those who have not heard can believe. Matthew 3:1–2 announces that John the Baptist came to proclaim repentance, for the kingdom was near.

Preaching is the proclamation of the good news that Jesus Christ is Lord. In most Protestant congregations, preaching or proclaiming is central. Congregants listen attentively weekly as the preacher provides comfort, encouragement, and instruction.

When most people think of *kerygma*, they think of someone who preaches in a formal congregational setting, but proclamation also includes Christians being witnesses to the good news of Jesus Christ to those around them. When believers share the good news with others, either through their daily witness or by telling the story of the gospel, they are engaged in proclamation.

Both the formal and the informal aspects of *kerygma* provide opportunities for faith to grow as members of faith communities are challenged and called to a life of love of God and neighbor. Through proclamation, lives are shaped and formed, and as a result, people's faith grows and they are nurtured as Christlike followers.

Mission and Service (Diakonia)

After Christians gather for worship, they are sent into the world to engage in mission and service. *Diakonia* means "service" or "ministry." The term is used in the New Testament to refer to all followers of Jesus Christ. All members of the body of Christ are to "serve" or "minister to" one another (1 Pet. 4:10). Ephesians 4:11–13 states that church leaders are to equip the saints for the work of ministry/service (*diakonia*) in order to expand and strengthen the body of Christ. This passage focuses on the diverse gifts in the body of Christ that are needed to serve the church and the kingdom of God. As members of a faith community live out community together, the gifts of the body of Christ become evident and the body of Christ is built up and equipped for God's mission in the world.

The mission of God (*mission Dei*) reflects the pattern of the triune God as captured in the words of Jesus: "As the Father has sent me, even so I am sending you" (John 20:21). God the Father sent Jesus Christ to redeem all humanity and creation. Jesus sent the Holy Spirit to empower and guide humans. And the triune God sent the church into the world to participate in the new creation. God has a mission in the world, and he calls, gathers, and sends the church into the world to participate in that mission. God exists as a missional God, and the church is to follow where God is already active in the world.[38]

The church is a sent people, responding to the call of Christ and empowered by the Holy Spirit to go into all nations. The church witnesses to the lordship of Christ and participates with God in the building of the kingdom of God (Matt. 28:19–20). The church is an instrument of God's mission for the redemption of all creation. Through Christians' participation in God's mission, God seeks to restore and redeem all creation.

Through mission and service, people become more compassionate toward others and more empathetic to their needs. As faith communities engage in service to their communities through food drives, service projects, mission trips, community gardens, and counseling services, they help Christians grow in their faith as they express their love of neighbor.

Justice (Propheteia)

While faith formation takes place primarily through worship, fellowship, and service, it also includes the prophetic voice advocating against the injustices of society. Faith formation takes place as Christians are moved to acts of compassion or works of mercy in order to express love for their neighbor. Throughout the Old Testament, prophets admonished wickedness, confronted injustice, and spoke against the sins of the people.

The call to justice includes advocating for someone who is being oppressed or is experiencing injustice. As Micah 6:8 states, we are "to do justice, and to love kindness, and to walk humbly with your God." Christians who engage in justice understand the importance of reaching their community for Christ by participating in ways to end injustice.

Jesus reflects this prophetic call to justice in Luke 4:18–19, quoting from Isaiah 61:1–2: "The Spirit of the Lord is upon me, because he has anointed me to proclaim good news to the poor. He has sent me to proclaim liberty to the captives and recovering of sight to the blind, to set at liberty those who are oppressed, to proclaim the year of the Lord's favor." Christians are to participate with God in the liberation of the poor, the captive, and the blind.

Justice is often expressed through such movements as liberation theology, feminist theology, and black theologies. These theological movements express the need for liberation of and freedom for particular people groups who have been oppressed. These theologies are less about doctrine and articles of faith and more about the current experiences of oppressed people. They focus on the fact that God identifies with and cares about the pain and suffering of God's people.

| Conclusion

A person's faith is dynamically developed, shaped, and transformed as they participate in a faith community. While the practices themselves do not form a person into Christlikeness, God's grace and their participation in communal practices create space for the Holy Spirit to work.

Worship is the primary center of faith formation in congregations as Christians gather to praise, read Scripture, hear the Word preached, and participate in Communion. Through the liturgy and weekly rituals of the church, the story of the gospel is narrated, and Christians find their identity in the retelling of the story. Christians are made new through baptism as a mark of dying to sin and being resurrected into new life, whether as an infant or as an adult. For Protestants, Communion and baptism are the essential sacraments in which Christians encounter God's presence and receive grace.

Local faith communities have a variety of practices that form faith in the lives of Christians, but some of the most impactful include fellowship through small groups, mission and service, proclamation, and justice. As Christians become present to one another through fellowship and small groups, they develop friendships and safe places to explore their faith and to live in community. As Christians go into the world to love their neighbor by engaging in acts of compassion and mercy, their faith is being formed to love others more deeply. And finally, as Christians advocate for the poor, oppressed, and marginalized of society, they participate in the very nature of God, who favors the poor and the oppressed. Their faith is strengthened as they love the outcasts of society. Through these communal practices, space is opened for Christians to experience God's grace and to be formed into Christlike followers. Faith formation in community is so important because Christians cannot grow in faith without one another and without participating in the practices of faith communities, where God's grace is freely offered.

Discussion Questions

1. What is the meaning of Horace Bushnell's Christian nurture for families and congregations?
2. How does John Westerhoff's definition of *catechesis* relate to the role the faith community plays in fostering faith formation?
3. What aspects of worship are necessary for people to be formed and shaped into Christlikeness?
4. What are some of the significant practices that foster faith formation in congregations?
5. What roles do mission, service, and justice play in faith formation in community?

| Further Reading

Duck, Ruth C. *Worship for the Whole People of God: Vital Worship for the 21st Century*. Louisville: Westminster John Knox, 2013.

Everist, Norma Cook. *The Church as Learning Community: A Comprehensive Guide to Christian Education*. Nashville: Abingdon, 2002.

Foster, Charles. *Educating Congregations: The Future of Christian Education*. Nashville: Abingdon, 1994.

Matthaei, Sondra Higgins. *Formation in Faith: The Congregational Ministry of Making Disciples*. Nashville: Abingdon, 2008.

Murphy, Debra Dean. *Teaching That Transforms: Worship as the Heart of Christian Education*. Grand Rapids: Brazos, 2004.

Nelson, C. Ellis. *Growing Up Christian: A Congregational Strategy for Nurturing Disciples*. New York: Paulist Press, 1983.

Westerhoff, John, III. *Living the Faith Community: The Church That Makes a Difference*. Minneapolis: Winston Press, 1985.

7

The Role of Scripture in
Faith Formation

The significant role that congregational life and its rituals and practices play in faith formation was illustrated in the previous chapter. Central to these rituals and practices is Scripture, making an appropriation of Scripture vital to faith formation. Since the Bible is central to a Christian's life of faith and practice, reading, studying, and reflecting on Scripture are necessary both individually and corporately.

Christians read Scripture as a means to understand how God has worked throughout history and how God is at work in the world today. Scripture is an essential resource for defining the character and content of faith formation and Christian practice. The writers of Scripture were persuaded that God had made himself known to them in the events and words they reported, and they were convinced that God had moved them to write for the spiritual benefit of their readers. This is what is meant by divine revelation and inspiration. Scripture's work is incomplete until the Spirit inspires the reader of the Bible to accept its message as the revelation of Christ to them personally and communally.[1] The Bible is "inspired" as a means to form Christian character and Christlike living. As 2 Timothy 3:16–17 says, "All scripture is inspired by God and is useful for teaching, for reproof, for correction, and for training in righteousness, so that everyone who belongs to God may be proficient, equipped for every good work" (NRSV).

The fact that Scripture is "inspired" means that the authority of the Bible is not found in individual parts but in the whole of Scripture. Broadly speaking, evangelical Christians refer to this as a "plenary" interpretation of Scripture, meaning that to view Scripture in isolated proof texts can be problematic. It also means that all Scripture is God-breathed. A proper understanding of the story of Scripture involves reading and understanding the overall narrative of its content. Scripture is a divine-human book. God inspired human authors to write the Bible in a particular historical context. As Christians read, study, and reflect on Scripture, they seek to understand God and God's activity in the world through this divine-human medium. It is through Scripture that Christians seek to allow the Holy Spirit to form and transform them into Christlikeness.

Scripture as *Formation,* Not *Information*

While Christians affirm that Scripture is inspired and provides everything necessary for matters of salvation, faith, and Christian practice, many Christians continue to struggle to read the Bible and make application to their daily lives. Many Christians see the Bible as boring, complicated, and difficult to understand. The result is that many Christians don't read the Bible or take time to allow Scripture to form their faith.

A recent survey by LifeWay Research indicates that while nine out of ten households own Bibles, with most having at least three per household, only about half of Americans (53 percent) have read relatively little of the Bible. One out of ten has read none of it, while 13 percent of Americans have read a few sentences. Thirty percent say they have read several passages or stories.[2] The Pew Research Center indicates that 35 percent of Christians read the Bible occasionally, and 45 percent seldom or never read the Bible.[3] While these statistics are not encouraging, they are a reminder that while Christians affirm the authority of Scripture, many are not appropriating the Bible as a means of faith formation.

While some Christians suggest that postmodernism, secularization, and consumerism have affected Christian devotion, and while this may be true, another reason why Christians don't read the Bible is because of the way they have been taught to study Scripture. Most Christians have been taught that one reads Scripture primarily as a means of gaining information for apologetics, doctrine, or theological debate. In other words, Christians study Scripture to gain facts, to prove things, or to develop beliefs. Many in the field of biblical studies refer to this as a historical-critical approach to biblical studies. The primary goal of understanding the meaning of Scripture is to understand what is behind the text in its historical context. To understand what Scripture means today, one must know what Scripture meant in its historical context. The difficulty with this approach is that unless one is a biblical scholar or has knowledge about historical interpretation, one will not be able to properly understand the meaning of Scripture. Many Christians give up on reading the Bible because they haven't been taught how to interpret Scripture correctly. It could be that many Christians are not appropriating the Bible as a means of faith formation because of the past two hundred years of traditional biblical scholarship. While rigorous study of Scripture based on the historical-critical method is beneficial for biblical studies, it is limited when it comes to engaging the Bible for faith formation.

One of the questions that needs to be addressed is, What is the primary purpose of Scripture? Some Christians argue that the primary purpose of Scripture is to provide propositional truths or knowledge, while others state that the purpose of Scripture is to provide the story of God.[4] To answer this question, we need to ascertain the role of the Bible within the context of the church.

The common assumption is that the Christian canon exists so that one may assess the validity of Christian doctrine by what the Bible states—that is, the Bible functions to clarify theological *information* about the Christian faith. However, the canonical process itself suggests that the incorporation of the biblical texts into the Christian canon had more to do with their *formative* rather than their epistemic role.[5] In other words, the early church appropriated and turned repeatedly to this particular collection of texts because of the formative ways that these texts (and not others) functioned within the Christian community.[6] There are three distinct but related ways one may further clarify this understanding of the role of Scripture.[7]

First, an understanding of the formative role of Scripture suggests that there is more to the interpretive process than the discovery of a historical meaning contained in the biblical text. Contrary to many interpretive ventures (particularly traditional, text-centered approaches), the criterion for the perception of these biblical texts as authoritative Scripture is not merely what these texts state (i.e., the information in these texts) but what these texts do (i.e., the ways these texts function to affect their readers). As important as the biblical texts themselves may be, something essential—beyond the information in the texts—must happen within readers so that these texts become Scripture. There must be a convergence between the texts and their readers that brings those otherwise dead words to life.[8]

Second, an understanding of the formative role of Scripture suggests that the church is the location where these texts may function authoritatively. In significant ways, the Christian Scriptures themselves are related in the canonical process to the so-called rule of faith, which assumes the confessional context within which the reading and interpretation of these texts were expected to occur. These basic core theological convictions contributed to the formation of both the Christian canon and the faith community that turned to these specific texts as sacred Scripture.

Third, an understanding of the formative role of Scripture suggests the necessity of the performance or living out of the church's engagement with these texts as Scripture. The basic standard by which the functional role of Scripture within the church is evaluated focuses on the reception of and the response to these texts in the ongoing life of the faithful Christian community.

A historical understanding of the primary purpose of Scripture is significant because it reminds Christians that the reason Scripture is authoritative is because it was appropriated within the church. The Bible was given to the church not as a means of developing doctrine or belief but as a means for Christians to encounter the living God. Scripture was given to the church not for *information* but as a means of *formation*. As Barbara E. Bowe writes, "The Bible is not only a fundamental source of Christian spirituality; it is also a touchstone by which we discern the authenticity of all spirituality within the Christian community."[9]

The Nature of Formational Reading

Since the Bible was given to the church as a means of faith formation, we need to relearn how to read Scripture in more *subjective* ways, as opposed to the more *objective* academic or historical-critical approaches. While biblical scholarship has an important role to play in biblical interpretation, particularly when it comes to using tools and methodologies to understand what the text meant in its historical context, such an approach to Scripture does not automatically lead to faith formation. Instead, the reader is transformed by the influence of the Word of God, which is mediated through the words of the text by the power of the Holy Spirit.

The formative role of Scripture affirms that just as the Holy Spirit was active in inspiring the original authors of the Bible, the Holy Spirit is active in inspiring the people who read the text today. Some Bible scholars refer to this as double inspiration. As a person reads the Bible, the Holy Spirit inspires them to discern the will of God and to discover God and his ongoing work of salvation. Therefore, given that the Bible functions in formative ways, Christians are to consistently read and engage these sacred texts. And as they do, they move from viewing the Bible primarily as a source of information to experiencing the formative power of Scripture that transforms their lives.

Since Scripture is formative in nature, any person, regardless of their level of biblical expertise, can read the Bible and encounter God. In this regard, formational reading involves opening oneself up to the text to allow the Bible to intrude into one's life so one can be addressed by it. Instead of mastering the text through study, readers, through formational reading, invite the text to master and form them. Faithful readers approach the text open to hear, to receive, to respond, and to serve. Sandra Schneiders asserts that biblical spirituality indicates a transformative process of the individual and communal engagement with the biblical text. The nonspecialist can approach the text not merely as a historical record or even as a literary medium but as the Word of God.[10] When Christians read the Bible for formation, they find new excitement and energy in the text that they once viewed as boring and irrelevant.

Using the imagery that Jeremiah employs, the reader must continue to "eat these words."[11] Jeremiah states, "Your words were found, and I ate them, and your words became to me a joy and the delight of my heart, for I am called by your name, O LORD, God of hosts" (Jer. 15:16). The image of eating the words of Scripture invites the reader to let the text confront them. If the reader does, then the Word will continue to nourish, challenge, disturb, and encourage them. Jeremiah suggests that the reader eat the words in order to assimilate and make the words their own. Eating suggests that the reader tastes and savors both the bitter and the sweet and learns from each the wisdom that it holds. Eating means that the reader ingests slowly, carefully ruminating over the words they have eaten in their heart and mind.[12]

In light of eating the words of Scripture and digesting them, Robert Mulholland provides the following explanation for reading Scripture for formation rather than for information.

First, in contrast to reading for information, when reading for formation, the objective is not to cover as much as possible as quickly as possible. The reader is not concerned with getting through the Bible but with the quality of the reading. Formational reading takes longer and requires the reader to stop and reflect on what is being read.

Second, while informational reading is linear, with the reader trying to move quickly over the surface of the text, formational reading is deep. The reader seeks to allow a passage to open them up to its deeper dimensions, its multiple layers of meaning. The reader allows the text to become the intrusion of the Word of God into their life so it can address them and encounter them at deeper levels of their being.

Third, with informational reading, the reader seeks to master the text, but formational reading allows the text to master the reader. The reader approaches the text with an openness to hear, to receive, to respond, and to be a servant of the Word rather than a master of the text.

Fourth, instead of the text being an object the reader controls and manipulates according to their own insight and purposes, the text becomes the subject of the reading relationship; the reader is the object that is shaped by the text. Formational reading requires waiting before the text, spending time ruminating with the text in order to hear what the text is saying.

Fifth, while informational reading usually uses an analytical, critical, judgmental approach, formational reading requires a humble, detached, receptive, loving approach. Such an approach requires a radical reorientation of the inner posture of the reader. It is here where the reader begins to hear the call to spiritual disciplines of a deeper order.

Sixth, informational reading requires a problem-solving mentality. In contrast, formational reading requires an openness to mystery. In formational reading, the reader becomes open to the mystery that is God. The reader stands before that mystery and allows that mystery to address them.[13]

Reading Scripture for formation is a discipline that takes time to develop. While informational reading is something the reader can do more quickly, formational reading requires the reader to take time to "center down," to become still, to listen, and to wait to encounter the mystery of God.

What are some guidelines that will help the reader engage in formational reading on a regular basis? What are some practical ways to ensure that the reader has a holistic, disciplined approach to reading Scripture? John Wesley, the founder of Methodism, provides these practical guidelines for the reading of Scripture.

- *Daily reading.* The reader should set apart time from the pressures and tension of life for the daily reading of Scripture. This time should be when the reader is at their best, and the physical surrounding should be conducive to the opening of the reader's life to God.
- *Regular feeding.* When reading the Bible, the reader should include all of Scripture. The lectionary can be a great tool to ensure that the whole of Scripture is read.
- *Spiritual attitude.* When reading Scripture, the reader should be focused on listening to and knowing the whole will of God.
- *Prayer.* Prayer helps the reader to be open and receptive to encountering the living Word and ready to respond obediently to God.

• *Response.* As the reader reads Scripture, there should be an encounter and a response. There should be an examination of the reader's heart and an application to their life.[14] Wesley says, "While we read, we frequently pause, and examine ourselves by what we read, both with regard to our hearts and lives. . . . And whatever light you then receive should be used to the uttermost, and that immediately. Let there be no delay. Whatever you resolve, begin to execute the first moment you can."[15]

Engaging the Bible for Faith Formation

There are a variety of practices that can help a Christian engage the biblical text as a means of faith formation. Sarah Schneiders suggests five such practices.[16]

Hear the preaching of the Word of God. Scripture testifies that during Jesus's ministry, preaching touched many people, and their lives were transformed (Acts 2:37–41; 8:26–39). In preaching, the pastor mediates between sacred Scripture and those they serve in their context.[17]

Participate in liturgy or worship. Weekly liturgy includes songs, responses, rituals, prayers, Communion, and baptism. When the liturgy is celebrated by congregants, the enactment of God in symbol and song becomes a powerful method for people to experience personal and communal transformation.[18]

Take part in a small group. The value of small groups is that the biblical text is read together by people who share the same context. Reading Scripture in community works against the privatized and individualistic view of spirituality that is often present when people read Scripture. When Scripture is read in groups with people of different genders, ethnicities, and economic backgrounds, diverse voices contribute to an understanding of the text. Reading and studying Scripture in a small group helps people broaden and deepen their understanding of a given passage while guarding against misleading and individual interpretation. In a group setting, people talk about Scripture together, which helps them apply what they are learning in their lives.

Practice transformation in the world. This can include those who are privileged in society struggling to incorporate justice into society on behalf of those less privileged. It is one thing to hear the Word and another to act on the Word through compassion and justice.

Practice lectio divina. Lectio divina is a process that begins with slowing down, sitting quietly, and centering attention on the text. It is a process of spiritual encounter that includes a series of dynamics that move the reader to a deep level of engagement with a chosen text and with the Spirit, who enlivens the text. The steps include the following:

1. The first step is *silencio* ("silence"). The reader approaches the passage with open, receptive listening while reading silently. The reader then takes time for silent prayer.

2. The second step is *lectio* ("reading"). The reader reads the text aloud, slowly and deliberately, to evoke their imagination. Hearing the text reminds the hearer of the spoken Word of God. Often the text is committed to memory during this process.

3. The third step is *meditatio* ("meditation"). For a period of time, the reader meditates on, thinks about, or mentally chews on what has been read. This step often includes committing the text to memory. By internalizing the text in its verbal form, the reader continues to ruminate on the text's meaning.

4. The fourth step is *oratio* ("prayer"). The reader prays or responds to God, who speaks in and through the text. Praying is talking to God as one would to another person within a close relationship. The reader speaks to God aloud or writes the prayer in a journal.

5. The fifth step is *contemplatio* ("contemplation"). The reader rests silently before God, receiving whatever the Spirit gives. It is here that the reader is in union with God through the Spirit. This step might involve studying the text with the help of commentaries, reading the text in the context of the liturgy so as to encounter other biblical texts from both Testaments that the church sees as related, or using other forms of study that open the mind to the meaning of the passage. The purpose of *contemplatio* is deepened understanding of the text's meaning in the context of the reader's own life and experience.[19]

6. The sixth step is *compassio* ("compassion"). This step is the fruit of the contemplation of God as love—love of God and neighbor. Whatever insight, feeling, or commitment emerges from this time with Scripture is to be shared as grace with others.[20]

Lectio divina (Latin for "divine reading") is a practice that can be traced back to the desert fathers and mothers, whose spirituality consisted primarily of prayerful rumination on biblical texts.[21] This practice was later developed by the Benedictine monasteries ordered around the Rule of St. Benedict (c. 540). It was also practiced by John Calvin and the Puritan pastor Richard Baxter, who advocated a method of reflective meditation on Scripture that was directly derived from Benedictine practice.[22] Many Christians and faith communities are realizing the significance of this ancient practice as a means to make Bible reading exciting and engaging once again and to connect to the rich historical tradition of the church. Christians read Scripture not just as individuals but as participants in the broader Christian community throughout time.

Lectio divina can be done individually or corporately. The added advantage of group *lectio divina* is that what the reader hears can be immediately discussed with others who are listening to God. It also creates space for public intentions to be known, and the group can hold the person accountable. The group process also gives the reader an opportunity to become more familiar with the practice. Whether individually or in community, many Christians are rediscovering this ancient practice and incorporating it into their daily lives (see the *lectio divina* exercise at the end of this chapter for an example).

One of the common concerns about formational reading or *lectio divina* is that it can be very subjective. It is rightly criticized for answering only, What does this passage mean to me? What it meant in its original context may be ignored. In other words, it is often criticized for allowing people to stray from the original meaning of the passage. On the other hand, as discussed at the beginning of this chapter, an overemphasis on reading Scripture as an academic exercise based on a variety of interpretations can often leave the reader without a personal application regarding how they are to live.

Richard Peace's book *Contemplative Bible Reading: Experiencing God through Scripture* combines the benefits of both an analytical and a contemplative reading of Scripture. He suggests that the reader should study a passage twice. The first time involves serious Bible study in which the reader tries to understand what the text is saying—in other words, what the text meant in its original context. The second session then builds on this insight and by means of *lectio divina* invites the reader to listen with their heart to what their head knows. This study attempts to give the reader a balanced experience of the Bible that takes seriously the need to analyze and the need to listen, the need to understand and the need to pray.[23]

Peace's proposal can be a helpful avenue in combining analytical and contemplative practices in Bible study. Ideally, how the reader encounters the text, guided by the Holy Spirit, should result in both approaches being a means of faith formation. The challenge is not to allow the more analytical approach—an approach that we are most familiar with—to dominate the study process and in doing so minimize the more formational reading of the text.

Conclusion

For most readers of Scripture, the shift from informational to formational reading requires the development of new ways to appropriate Scripture in their lives. Most Christians have been taught to read Scripture as a means of gaining propositional truth, belief, and doctrine, or to master the text, but formational reading creates space for the text to master the reader. The reason Scripture was given to the church, and what makes Scripture authoritative, is that it forms and shapes people into Christlikeness. Faith formation through Scripture provides the reader with an opportunity to be enlivened by the Holy Spirit through their encounter with the text. Formational reading requires the reader to develop a daily habit of "eating the Word." This regular eating comes through practices such as small groups, Bible studies, and *lectio divina*. As Christians continue to engage in these practices, whether individually or corporately, they experience the transformative power of Scripture reading.

Discussion Questions

1. What are the differences between viewing Scripture as *information* and as *formation?* Why do these differences matter in regard to faith formation?
2. What are some meaningful Scripture practices you could use to form your faith?
3. What can you learn from John Wesley about daily practices of reading Scripture?
4. In what ways can you apply the practice of *lectio divina* in your faith formation and in the faith formation of others?
5. How can you keep the balance between reading Scripture analytically and contemplatively?

Further Reading

Benner, David G. *Opening to God: Lectio Divina and Life as Prayer.* Downers Grove, IL: InterVarsity, 2010.

Bowe, Barbara E. *Biblical Foundations of Spirituality: Touching a Finger to the Flame.* Lanham, MD: Sheed and Ward, 2003.

Mulholland, M. Robert. *Shaped by the Word: The Power of Scripture in Spiritual Formation.* Nashville: Upper Room, 1985.

Peace, Richard. *Contemplative Bible Reading: Experiencing God through Scripture.* Eugene, OR: Wipf & Stock, 2015.

Peterson, Eugene H. "Eat This Book: The Holy Community at Table with the Holy Scripture." *Theology Today* 56, no. 1 (1999): 5–17.

Lectio Divina Exercise

This exercise can be done individually or in a community setting.

Centering

Each person quiets the body and the mind. They relax, sit comfortably but alert, close their eyes, and attune to their breathing.

Listening for the Gentle Touch of Christ the Word (Literal Sense)

- *Silencio:* Take a couple minutes in silent meditation as you prepare to hear Scripture being read.
- *Lectio:* One person reads aloud Psalm 146.
- *Meditatio:* Take a couple minutes of silence to be attentive to a word that is especially meaningful.
- *Oratio:* Participants share aloud a simple statement of one word. No elaboration!
- *Contemplatio:* Take a few minutes to contemplate what you heard shared.

Listening a Second Time for the Gentle Touch of Christ the Word (Literal Sense)

- *Silencio:* Take a couple minutes in silent meditation as you prepare to hear Scripture being read.
- *Lectio:* A second person reads aloud Psalm 146.
- *Meditatio:* Take a couple minutes of silence to be attentive to a word that is especially meaningful.
- *Oratio:* Participants share aloud a simple statement of one word. No elaboration!
- *Contemplatio:* Take a few minutes to contemplate what you heard shared.

Determining How Christ the Word Speaks to Me (Allegorical Sense)

- *Silencio:* Take a couple minutes in silent meditation as you prepare to hear Scripture being read.
- *Lectio:* One person reads aloud Psalm 146.

- *Meditatio:* Take a couple minutes of silence to be attentive to a word that is especially meaningful.
- *Oratio:* Participants share aloud a simple statement of one word. No elaboration!
- *Contemplatio:* Take a few minutes to contemplate what you heard shared.

Determining What Christ the Word Invites Me to Do (Moral Sense)

- *Silencio:* Take a couple minutes in silent meditation as you prepare to hear Scripture being read.
- *Lectio:* One person reads aloud Psalm 146.
- *Meditatio:* Take a couple minutes of silence to be attentive to a word that is especially meaningful.
- *Oratio:* Participants share aloud a simple statement of one word. No elaboration!
- *Contemplatio:* Take a few minutes to contemplate what you heard shared.
- *Compassio:* Invite listeners to reflect: "I believe God wants me to . . . today/this week."

Prayer

Part 3

Global Dimensions of Faith Formation

8

Forming Faith through Missions

I n the ancient and medieval world, the average person, whether living in a city or a village, traveled only several miles from their home. Their world was limited, stable, predictable, and very familiar to them. It was small. Now we live by the notion that the world is getting smaller, closer, more interconnected. The limitations of a day's travel on foot no longer exist. We can be on the other side of the world instantaneously with videoconferencing technology or literally with a fifteen-hour flight. Our cultural context is no longer limited to just the one in which we live; it can expand around the globe. Faith formation in a global context is not just a wish, an ideal, or a theoretical possibility but a tangible reality that has actually been experienced by many believers through short-term mission trips.

Our culture—whatever culture in which we live—shapes our faith; it influences the formation of our faith. However, after some time, faith becomes content, comfortable within that context. It seeks a balance between faith and culture, establishing an equilibrium with the societal factors that influence the formation of faith. Faith formation can be stalled due to a lack of cultural stimuli to challenge, kindle, or excite it, which can be done only by a change of culture. Anyone who has had a cross-cultural experience in ministry, even for a short term, knows the influence it has on one's faith; you are never the same.

For example, while one of the authors was visiting believers in China several years ago, during a period when their government was exhibiting a more tolerant posture toward the practice of the Christian faith within China, they spoke of the previous generations' faith, which had flourished even under relentless censorship and active persecution, as being so much stronger, more robust than theirs. These believers noted that having grown up in a different period, one decisively different from that of their parents, their faith was different. It was far more expressive but not as resilient due to the change in culture and the absence of those factors that had contributed to the resiliency. They defined and expressed faith differently in part due to their distinct cultural context. Now with the unfortunate renewal of a more suspicious posture toward Christianity by the Chinese government, faith will once again change—as will the how, when, why, and where it is formed. Imagine how your faith would change, both inwardly and outwardly, in the formative process and how that process was displayed, if you were in a different cultural context, one more repressive than your own or one more conducive to faith.

Doing Ministry for Faith Formation

Previous chapters discussed how faith is made evident by works. However, it is just as crucial to see that works also contribute to the formation of faith. Scripture affirms that our deeds are not just of temporal value but follow us into eternity (1 Cor. 3:8; 2 Cor. 5:10; Rev. 13:14). They also provide a tangible reminder of our repentance (Matt. 3:8; Luke 3:8) and our kingdom citizenship (Matt. 7:15–20). Not only do our deeds demonstrate our faith in fulfilling God's will (Rom. 2:6), demonstrating our acceptance by God (Acts 10:34–35), but they also protect us from the forces of darkness (Rom. 13:12). As our faith becomes habitual, it results in a Christian life that includes deeds (Titus 2:6–8), and these deeds contribute to the formation of faith.

However, most importantly, particularly in light of participating in cross-cultural, short-term mission trips, deeds are not simply done for our own good but to minister to others in need (Titus 3:14). This simple observation perhaps goes unnoticed when studying the apparent difference between Paul's and James's views of works in relation to saving faith. William Dyrness reminds us that in James we must conceive what deeds/works mean against the context of the beginning of James 2 and the close of James 2, specifically, how verse 8 explains verses 15–16: "Works are giving to a brother or sister what they need. It is, in a word, the gift of hospitality, an open giving of yourself and your goods to the needy."[1] Faith becomes a matter of who it benefits: self or others? If it focuses on self, James raises the rhetorical question, "Can that faith save him?" (v. 14). But if it is focused on others (vv. 15–16), it harkens back to the care of widows and orphans, true religion (1:27). There is a purpose to faith. It is not profitable by itself (2:17) but only if it serves others. This understanding of faith and deeds in James 2:14–18 must be seen in light of 2:1–13. James is saying what our salvation should do. Table 8.1 demonstrates the parallel between what James describes as a Christian's responsibilities to those in need and what he later would teach regarding the relationship between faith and works, which often goes unnoticed in many commentaries and translations.

Table 8.1
Works for Others, Not for Self

James 2:1–13	James 2:14–18
My brothers . . . faith (2:1)	My brothers . . . faith (2:14)
The poor person in filthy clothes (2:2)	A brother or sister ill-clad and lacking in daily sustenance (2:15)
The poor . . . wealthy in faith . . . [who] love God (2:5)	Faith . . . works (ten times in thirteen verses)
You are doing right [*kalōs*, καλῶς] (2:8)	Excellent! [*kalōs poieis*, καλῶς ποιεῖς] (2:19)
The fine name by which you have been called (2:7)	[Abraham] was called God's friend (2:23)

Source: Ralph P. Martin, *James*, Word Biblical Commentary 48 (Waco: Word, 1988), 78–79.

Short-term mission trips, which are indeed works of faith, should minister to the needs of others, especially those who are less fortunate spiritually and physically. Yet in the end, the experience also has a profound impact on the faith of those doing the work itself. The experience of a short-term mission trip activates many of the tangible benefits of the faithful, selfless service described in Scripture.

Biblical Precedent for Cross-Cultural Missions and Faith Formation

After his resurrection, after three years discipling and training the disciples to be world missionaries, Jesus explained to them, "It is not for you to know times or seasons that the Father has fixed by his own authority. But you will receive power when the Holy Spirit has come upon you, and you will be my witnesses in Jerusalem and in all Judea and Samaria, and to the end of the earth" (Acts 1:7–8). Jesus had prepared his disciples to go from their homes in Galilee by taking them throughout the region for three years, taking them into the territories of the Samaritans and gentiles so they would be ready to be his witnesses in other nations. Jesus had not just trained them to do the work of ministry; he had expanded their faith to accept the call to global missions.

Jim Putman, pastor of Real Life Ministries in Post Falls, Idaho, and expert in the area of discipleship, explored how Jesus discipled his followers so they would become world changers, with a faith that transcended their own context so they could reach those who were different, the "other," even those they had been told never to associate with. Putman identifies six principles in this regard:

1. Jesus brought them to a place/situation where there were people who were in need.
2. Jesus taught them.
3. Jesus connected them to God and to each other.
4. Jesus equipped them and released them to do ministry.
5. Jesus shared truth that was new to them.
6. Jesus modeled discipleship to them as they were all together.[2]

Jesus's journey with the disciples was not designed for expediency but for instruction, not to isolate them culturally but to expand their horizons, not to coddle them but to stretch them and their faith so they could accomplish the Great Commission. Jesus took his disciples through the gentile region of the Decapolis as well as through Samaria, where those who were only part Jewish lived. There an encounter with a woman of ill repute at the town well challenged the status quo of the disciples' faith. Their faith would have to grow so as to convey them on the path of discipleship.

Stephen Fortosis and Ken Garland studied the occurrences of cognitive disequilibration throughout the Scriptures, noting the occasions when the cultural status quo had to be changed in order to stretch the understanding (and faith) of the individuals within the text. They had to be put in a challenging situation in which standard responses would not apply. One occasion when this happened was with the Samaritan woman at the well in John 4. "In this account of Jesus's conversation with the Samaritan woman, disequilibration is clear. By simply speaking to her in public, Jesus disequilibrated her since such conversations violated numerous religious and cultural rules."[3] The same could be said for the disciples, who likewise were being drawn from their cultural comfort zones. "Just then his disciples came back. *They marveled that he was talking with a woman*, but no one said, 'What do you seek?' or, 'Why are you talking with her?'" (John 4:27). The disciples experienced disequilibration as well, but they adapted and grew to embrace even a Samaritan woman of questionable character.

Fortosis, in another article, applies the principle of disequilibration to the formation of faith. He articulates a theological basis for faith formation utilizing the notable New Testament character Simon Peter as a model for one's faith formation. While he identifies many transitions in the life of Peter, the three that most apply to the impact of short-term mission trips are "egocentrism to self-transcendence," "conditional love to compassion with others," and "fluid convictions to internalized convictions."[4] Peter's faith transformation was in part facilitated by the expanding of his world from a fishing village in Galilee to the imperial capital of Rome.

The Principle of Cognitive Dissonance and Faith Formation

James encourages his readers, "Count it all joy, my brothers, when you meet trials of various kinds, for you know that the testing of your faith produces steadfastness. And let steadfastness have its full effect, that you may be perfect and complete, lacking in nothing" (1:2–4). While no one wants to encounter trials, what if a "trial" or a faith challenge could be facilitated in a controlled environment?

Engagement in short-term mission trips provides this experience, becoming the catalytic event for faith formation to transpire. The most significant work done in recent years on the subject is *Transformission: Making Disciples through Short-Term Missions* by Michael S. Wilder and Shane W. Parker.[5] Based on the theory of cognitive dissonance postulated by the late Leon Festinger of Stanford University, Wilder and Parker explain how participation in cross-cultural encounters creates a never-before-encountered sense of ambiguity and confusion. People then have to contend with the inconsistency between their beliefs, values, and actions—that is, dissonance—seeking to return to balance and consistency. In short, the disharmony people experience confronts their desire for consistency, creating tension until harmony and consistency are reasserted. Wilder and Parker surmise that short-term missions are a means of "making them uncomfortable" and "support for stirring up dissonance,"[6] providing a robust context for faith formation. Terence Linhart illustrates this in an account of a youth group's mission trip: "The students were commissioned to act on their discernment during their encounters, embarking on a spiritual journey that transpired in a foreign culture where they did not know the language or customs. *The learning emerged from the steps of faith they took as they acted on their knowledge.* The result, then, was that the culture removed the familiar markers of existence and *the students developed a deeper faith in God.*"[7]

In discussing adolescent development, Fortosis and Garland note that one of the most influential factors in cognitive development is participation in a cross-cultural experience, whether in an urban, domestic, or international setting.[8] Based on a study of the influence of short-term mission trips on faith formation conducted by P. L. Benson and C. H. Eklin,[9] Stephen T. Beers reports that while there were few quantitatively significant results, the qualitative benchmarks "showed growth in six of the eight core dimensions of faith."[10] The three most notable factors are "sensitivity to cultural diversity," "sense of well-being," and "connection with a community of believers."[11] While these factors are part of a normal progression of faith formation, they seemed to be accentuated in the context of a cross-cultural mission trip.

Dissonance is more than cognitive; a holistic adjustment of identity is needed to restore harmony and consistency. A change of identity, one's concept of self, is most challenged by cross-cultural mission exposure. Linhart describes "the spectacle self" as the way in which our current sociocultural context identifies us—that is, part of our identity is bound up in how our own culture labels or values us. A Christian adolescent (or even an emerging adult) has an identity shaped by a relationship with a significant other, an athletic team, musical preferences or group, club or societal participation, political affinity, not to mention the value-based demographic perceptions of rich/poor, north/south, urban/rural. However, when they are removed from their own culture and immersed into a cross-cultural experience, the assumptions of who they are, their identity, become very fluid and must be redefined internally rather than by their context. This is their *real* self, including their ethics and vocation passion.[12]

For example, the high school football player from rural central Missouri who loves Toby Keith, is part of the Future Farmers of America (FFA), and values being a political conservative (e.g., Republican) and exercising his second amendment rights finds out that in Argentina none of this matters. It is all virtually irrelevant. They play fútbol (which is nothing like US football) and don't know anything about American country music or FFA. Likewise, his American political affiliation serves little if any purpose on an Argentinian mission trip, let alone a constitutional right he does not possess on foreign soil. Identity has to come from who we are, what we do, and ultimately who we worship, all of which centers on faith. The only common element between believers in the United States and believers in Argentina is faith in Christ. Suddenly, faith takes center stage in one's identity as all the other identity markers fade into irrelevance.

Faith Formation through Cross-Cultural Missions

Jim Henderson (a Christian) and Matt Casper (an atheist) began a dialogue about the church, including the nature of faith. *Jim and Casper Go to Church* describes Casper's negative reaction to the megachurch experience (lights, sound, special effects, massive screens—everything you'd need for a sporting event or a Hollywood production). He acknowledged he was more impressed by the congregation's outreach and mission work in Africa, valuing it far more than the sound and light show at the Sunday morning service.[13] Casper demonstrates that cross-cultural missions have an impact even on nonbelievers' perceptions of the Christian faith, possibly becoming a catalyst for their coming to faith in Christ.

In light of the discussion from Scripture as well as the insights from cognitive dissonance theory, the following specific faith formation outcomes have been identified.

Dependence on God. Rather than relying on more typical supports in life such as home, school, community, and family, when on a mission trip, even a short one, participants become aware of their increased dependence on God's provision, presence, and purpose for them. As they overcome their fears of living in an unfamiliar culture, they learn to lean on their faith for sustenance, becoming more God-centered than ever before. As one study concludes, "For the students, depending on the comfort zone for happiness and fulfillment equaled a lack of faith and dependence on God. They saw the desire to move beyond their fears and present their faith as a witness as one of the primary goals while on the trip."[14]

Tangible faith. Kurt Alan Ver Beek identifies the tangible results for participants of one mission trip: increased time spent in prayer and volunteering, financial giving, involvement in the congregation, interest in and advocacy for the poor (domestic and international), and increased interest in mission trips and kingdom work.[15] The gospel, rather than being regarded as a theological affirmation or message, is seen in changed lives, outreach, and ministry, making it more real and self-evident. In the words of James, "Show me your faith apart from your works, and I will show you my faith by my works" (2:18).

Experiential learning. Churches often talk about missions or share about their international mission partners. Congregations often have a mission month, a quarterly mission moment, or a missionary share in a service. However, there is a significant difference between the learning that takes place in a church setting and the learning that occurs by actively engaging in a cross-cultural mission experience. Short-term mission work makes missions real, part of a participant's faith experience.

Participation in God's work. The impact of taking an active part in sharing the faith, ministering to those in need, and expanding the kingdom of God is almost inestimable. There is a difference between supporting God's work and doing God's work. Doing God's work prioritizes servanthood rather than leadership,[16] and it can be a catalyst for identifying one's vocation, one's giftedness, and even God's calling on one's life.

Cross-cultural awareness. Cross-cultural experiences definitely challenge one's perceptions and values. Without a doubt, those who are aware of their own culture and are open to see other cultures have a wider worldview. In one study, a short-term mission outcome was "the participants' awareness of poverty. Students were affected by the disparity of wealth distribution within the host country and between the host country and their home culture."[17] Cross-cultural exposures broaden one's perspective and provide new opportunities for growth. While cross-cultural experiences challenge cultural assumptions, the same can be said regarding the assumptions of faith. People can grow in their faith as they are exposed to the faith of others, how it is articulated, and the habits associated with it.

Formative relationships. Formative relationships are also a benefit of short-term mission trips. In writing about the impact of a mission trip, Conrad Swartzentruber states, the "development of relationships included several groups of people, but students spoke most frequently of the impact from their relationships with children."[18] Through shared experiences, not only memories are made, but also life mentors are formed who are tied to the memories of impressionable events. There is a turn from focus on the self to focus on others—those from whom one can learn and those whom one can serve. Perhaps most significant is the relationship with the "other." Those who were previously unknown or marginalized are now known personally, and their expressions of faith and practices of faith formation are no longer regarded as foreign but as Christian.

Practices for Forming Faith through Missions

Terence Linhart's study of the impact of short-term mission trips on adolescent faith demonstrates that the effects last far beyond the end of the trip or even the typical reunion of participants after returning home.[19] In his *Christian Education Journal* article, Linhart suggests a five-step model for creating a curricular approach to short-term missions, one that will allow mission trips to have a lasting impact on participants.

1. Focus: anticipating the experience
2. Action-reflection: engaging in the experience
3. Support-feedback: sharing in the experience

4. Debrief: dissecting the experience

5. Learning transfer: linking the experience with life[20]

Here are some other practices that will maximize the impact of a short-term mission trip.

Prepare the team to experience the mission field. This is not a vacation! Providing practical skill training as well as resources for faith formation is crucial. In fact, for the most thorough training and preparation, some people even take part in an immersion experience in a cross-cultural environment. For example, Servants in Faith and Technology (SIFAT, www.sifat.org) in Lineville, Alabama, provides simulated exposures to cross-cultural mission destinations, down to the sights, smells, sounds, and challenges of daily living, such as cooking with a dung fire. They also help participants with applications of technology typically used on the mission field that can be utilized even after the actual mission trip is completed.

Use on-the-job training to equip people thoroughly for what they will be doing. This not only provides participants with the necessary skills, whether to do construction or lead a Bible study, but also builds a formative relationship with a more mature, seasoned mentor. This is an opportunity to learn by watching, to experience trial and error with feedback, and then to work while being supervised until the task can be performed independently.

Capitalize on the experience. Following the short-term mission experience, it is customary to have a celebration, not to mention a reunion sometime later (usually within two months), allowing families and the congregation to share vicariously in the experience with the team. However, to make sure the short-term experience translates into a long-term commitment and fuels faith formation, the congregation should capitalize on the experience. The congregation can study "doing good" in Scripture and determine the needs that exist in their own neighborhood. Members can study justice in regard to the county and state, applying the gospel not only to their lives but also to society. They can study social concepts from a Christian perspective and develop action plans to live out the faith. Such endeavors can take place within small groups and involve those who are going on the next mission trip.[21]

| Conclusion

"I'll never be the same again." This is a common response from adolescents and adults upon returning from a mission trip. Anyone who has ever participated in a cross-cultural experience or short-term mission trip knows this feeling. Such experiences often impact faith formation. Therefore, the church must create ongoing opportunities for these experiences, not only abroad but also at home. What is required is a *glocal* approach, led by those who think globally and act locally, whose faith is not limited to their own culture and society but genuinely transcends its confines and finds expression throughout human culture. Faith formation can happen through missions as people participate in God's ministry and mission wherever God plants them.

Discussion Questions

1. Has exposure to a different culture, even within your own country, impacted your faith? Benefited you? Challenged you?
2. Can you remember a period of cognitive dissonance in your own life? Explain its impact on your faith formation.
3. Stephen Fortosis writes of the transformation of Peter as he encountered Jesus. How would you describe specific elements of transformation in your own life?
4. How could you have a *glocal* perspective on life, ministry, and faith? Give specifics.

Further Reading

Ellis, Lynne, with Doug Fields. *Mission Trips from Start to Finish: How to Organize and Lead Impactful Mission Trips*. Loveland, CO: Group Publishing, 2008.

Maddix, Mark, and Jay Akkerman, eds. *Missional Discipleship: Partners in God's Redemptive Mission in the World*. Kansas City, MO: Beacon Hill, 2013.

Nouwen, Henri J. M., Donald P. McNeill, and Douglas A. Morrison. *Compassion: A Reflection on the Christian Life*. New York: Image Book by Doubleday, 2006.

Wilder, Michael S., and Shane W. Parker. *Transformission: Making Disciples through Short-Term Missions*. Nashville: B&H, 2010.

9

Faith Formation in Multiethnic Contexts

In a society that is becoming increasingly multiethnic, developing culturally relevant ministry depends on the recognition of the influence that culture has on faith formation. Although cultural analysis as an academic inquiry has served as a catalyst for Christian studies, the past theorists of faith formation have not adequately addressed the connection between culture and faith formation. Past theorists simply assumed that the connection was mutually exclusive.[1] While details have yet to be worked out, it seems safe to argue that the universality of these theories, let alone their validity, is problematic due to their relegating matters of faith to the isolated world of the individual. The relational dimension of culture, giving faith its stability and resilience, was largely ignored, and faith was reduced to a mere intellectual reception of the truth conceived within the private sphere of the Christian life. We need a holistic study that explains the connection between multiethnic culture and faith and offers a sound basis for guiding the church.

This chapter responds to the neglect of multiethnic Christian faith formation and contributes to debates on the relationship between faith and culture. Before continuing further, however, some explanations are needed. First, the word *faith* is a synonym for Christian faith, except when explicitly noted that it is being used otherwise. Many scholars use *faith* in a broader sense that includes various religious, philosophical, and ideological thoughts. The concept of faith used in this chapter is exclusively limited to the definition provided in chapter 3. Faith is God's grace-induced and the Holy Spirit–empowered assent given in knowledge of, belief in, and trust in Jesus Christ (Matt. 19:11; Luke 1:16; 7:43; John 16:13; Acts 4:32; Rom. 1:28; 8:14; Gal. 5:10; Eph. 2:8; 2 Tim. 2:25; Heb. 3:14). Along this line of thought, the term *multiethnic faith* is synonymous with multiethnic Christian faith. Second, in this chapter, *culture* is "an integrated system of learned patterns of behaviors, ideas, and products characteristic of a society."[2] As this definition suggests, there are social, ideological, and material elements to culture. The social element includes social structures, family relationships, holidays, traditions, food, and so forth. The ideological element includes norms, values, beliefs, symbols, and language. And the material element refers to the physical objects, tools, technology, clothes, and belongings that people pass from one generation to the next. Although the particulars of human culture may differ from one group to another, all cultures include these three basic elements. Third, this chapter relies on systematic theology as a binding system to review various cultural issues affecting faith formation because any discussions surrounding faith should be governed by the Bible's theological categories.

Understanding Human Culture: Theoretical Reflection

As a first step toward studying faith formation in multiethnic contexts, this section includes a theoretical reflection on public debates about human culture and seeks to bring some clarity to the theories of cultural diversity and adaptation.

In order to study how multiethnic culture affects faith formation, it is important to note some of the implicit assumptions that undergird cultural theories. Two assumptions dominate the discussion of culture. Some interpret culture as a *historical phenomenon* circumscribed to a region, while others regard it as a *social phenomenon* confined to an individual's experience. Those who hold to the historical view consider culture a set of fixed beliefs, values, and traditions based on regionality. They believe that culture is the historical construct that characterizes the life of a specific people group. However, those who endorse the social view interpret culture as a creative force in constant flux that has no regional specificity. They attempt to go beyond the visible and historical spheres of culture to the dynamic stream of time that contains a confluence of various ideologies. In essence, the proponents of the second view affirm culture as a social construct that takes on the subjective experiences of the individuals shaping it.

In social science, these historical and social assumptions became the basic premises from which cultural theories were developed. For example, the theories of multiethnicity and multiculturalism are based on a macro-scale analysis of culture taking place at the historical level, whereas the theories of assimilation and acculturation are based on a micro-scale analysis of culture taking place at the social level. The main difference among these theories is interpreting culture based on either historicity or social contingency.

Perspectives on Cultural Diversity: Multiethnicity versus Multiculturalism

In order to understand the relationship between cultural diversity and faith, we need to explore the theories of multiethnicity and multiculturalism—the sociological constructs that describe the presence of ethnic and cultural heterogeneity. The initial formulation of these concepts began in sociology, but today they are no longer confined to a single school of thought. They have become interdisciplinary subjects in the fields of education, philosophy, political science, history, business, psychology, church ministry, evangelism, and missions. Particularly in Christian studies, both concepts are employed in studying sociocultural factors affecting the formation of faith.

The theories of multiethnicity and multiculturalism are value-laden ideas open to various interpretations. Some Christians are skeptical of their value, while others view them as new ministry paradigms for the future. To a large degree, the disparity is due to the fact that a consistent definition of these terms does not exist in the literature. This confusion is further complicated by people's inconsistent use of the terms. Some people use both ideas as synonyms, while others use them as distinct concepts yet without a clear explanation of the distinction between them. Since people's unequivocal use of the terms has created confusion and misunderstanding, it is important to clarify what these terms mean.

From a purely theoretical point of view, multiethnicity is an idea that refers to a group of people having two or more sociohistorical heritages. As a system of value, the concept of multiethnicity represents heterogeneity as opposed to homogeneity. It is a system of thought that recognizes and responds to the presence of diverse people groups; the word *ethnicity* comes from the Greek word *ethnos* (ἔθνος), which means "people." *Ethnos* is a socially determined variable that indicates where and how a person was raised. Combined with the prefix *multi-*, the word *multiethnicity* indicates the state of being with people who have different sociohistorical identities, values, and traditions.

In the study of faith formation, multiethnicity is a valuable term that can help us understand that the body of Jesus Christ is comprised of people of various ethnic and sociocultural backgrounds. Theologically speaking, multiethnicity means recognizing ethnic diversity as a starting point of unity in Christ, not as a counterpoint. Such was the case with the church in Jerusalem (Acts 6:1–7) and in Antioch (Acts 11:19–30). A culturally diverse group of believers came together and created unity through their faith in Jesus Christ (Eph. 4:5–6).

While the concept of multiethnicity is often used in the discussion of cultural diversity these days, secular scholars, in general, prefer the term *multicultural-ism* instead. They believe that the multicultural idea accurately depicts the character and content of today's society. In sociological discourse, the concept of multiculturalism carries lexical and structural meanings. The lexical definition of multiculturalism is similar to that of multiethnicity in that it denotes an organization, society, or nation having two or more people groups. It acknowledges the value of ethnic diversity and promotes the continued contribution of all people in harmony. However, its structural definition, meaning how the term is used in public discourse, connotes ideological pluralism. The premise of relativism was established as the axiom of its tenets and functions as its principal criterion. As an example, the notion of multiculturalism promotes tolerance of various philosophical and religious ideas in public discourse. It challenges the existence of fixed borders of truth and asserts the multiplicity and relativity of truth based on people's subjective beliefs and experiences. This, in turn, rejects the totalizing and transcendent truth of philosophy, including the exclusivity of Christian truth. In brief, the notion of multiculturalism sends mixed messages. It connotes ethnic-cultural diversity and/or ideological pluralism, depending on how the term is used in public discourse. Since multiculturalism carries a wide array of meanings in public discourse, if at all possible, Christians should avoid using the term when describing cultural issues affecting faith. The connection between lexical and structural meanings is like two sides of a coin: we simply cannot separate the notions of diversity and pluralism from each other. Both meanings often go together in public discourse.

Perspectives on Cultural Adaptation: Assimilation versus Acculturation

Given the continuous demographic changes taking place nationally, understanding how people adapt to and cope with sociocultural changes is important even in church ministry. In the literature outlining what is currently known about individuals undergoing cultural adaptation, two ideas emerge: assimilation and acculturation. These concepts describe what happens to people's values and behaviors when two or more cultures come together for extended periods of time. The visual equivalent that corresponds to these ideas places assimilation on one end of a continuum with acculturation on the other end (see fig. 9.1).

Figure 9.1
Cultural adaptation

Assimilation ⟵═══⟶ **Acculturation**

In general, the assimilation theory explains a one-way process involving cultural imitation. It explains the process whereby people of a minority culture fully adopt the ways of the majority culture. It is like fusing subgroups into the dominant group, resulting in a new, homogeneous culture. However, a loss of minority culture takes place. The minority culture becomes indistinguishable from the majority culture in the process.

The acculturation theory, on the other hand, explains a two-way process involving cultural exchange. It explains the process whereby people of a minority culture absorb the cultural features common in the dominant culture while retaining their own culture. While sociological and psychological changes may occur, the native culture that people came from is not totally abandoned. Minority people are still able to retain their own cultural beliefs, values, and traditions. The outcome of the acculturation process is cultural pluralism.

There are two popular metaphors that are often used to describe assimilation and acculturation. They are the melting pot and cultural mosaic, respectively. The melting pot concept was used to describe cultural assimilation in colonial America in its early years. In an essay titled "Letters from an American Farmer" (1782), a French immigrant, Michel-Guillaume de Crevecoeur, first coined the term when he described how the colonial American society was being formed by men and women of diverse ethnic backgrounds. He described America as being a nation made up of people of various descent that would become a distinct nation with a culture that would greatly vary from the cultures of the motherlands. About 126 years later, the same metaphor was revisited by Israel Zangwill's stage play *The Melting Pot*, which depicted the life of David Quixano, a Russian Jew immigrant in search of a society free of racial and ethnic tensions. In the play, Zangwill used the term *melting pot* to depict how the fusion of cultures and the mingling of races would produce a homogeneous American society. In the United States, the concept of the melting pot has become a standard concept for describing people of diverse cultures producing a homogeneous society.

A popular metaphor for acculturation is the cultural mosaic. This metaphor describes a society that has numerous characteristics of different cultures. Subsumed within this metaphor is the recognition and the valuing of a collage of diverse worldviews, races, and ethnicities that make up a society and enrich people's lives. The idea of the cultural mosaic is based on a belief that the various races and ethnicities are central to the existence and continuation of a society. Similar to how a collage of decorative materials produces an exquisite image in a mosaic, the multiple cultures in a society interact and sustain one another in harmony. Here it is important to recognize that the mosaic metaphor insinuates an idea of multiculturalism—that society as a whole becomes stronger by having various cultural, ideological, and religious values.

When studying faith formation, less controversial terms are *multiethnicity*, *assimilation*, and *melting pot*. At first glance, however, even the notions of multiethnicity, assimilation, and the melting pot may seem to underestimate the power of the gospel to create a pathway toward Christian unity. They do not. These concepts are based on a descriptive theory, which explains "things as they actually are" rather than "what we want them to be." In other words, these concepts are not intended to be prescriptive in nature, as in the case of multiculturalism, adaptation, and the cultural mosaic, which have a postmodern agenda of promoting pluralism and relativism. The theories of multiethnicity, assimilation, and the melting pot are simple descriptors that explain the way culture manifests itself in the world and inform how we can make sense of our sociocultural reality.

A Biblical Basis for Diversity: Theological Reflection

The American demographic landscape is changing. Diversity is on the rise, with all racial and ethnic minority groups growing precipitously. The US Census Bureau reported that the non-white population is growing rapidly and could make up over 50 percent of the US population by the year 2040.[3] This means we will no longer sit in church pews surrounded by people of our own ethnic type. Churches will be largely made up of people of different ethnic heritages.

Changes in the landscape of our society are already causing many churches to reexamine the issue of diversity in light of biblical principles. Church leaders are in the midst of having unprecedented conversations about race, ethnicity, and diversity with the goal of creating a more inclusive ministry environment. They desire to implement a commitment to ethnic and cultural diversity, to promote racial reconciliation, and to advance intercultural understanding among church members. As local churches are becoming increasingly diverse, creating a more inclusive ministry environment has become a critical issue for the church today.

Despite many conversations taking place among church leaders, the primary basis of their discussion is largely social science. While understanding how social science theories make the case for valuing diversity is beneficial, Christians' primary view on diversity should be based on God's inerrant Word, the Bible. If the Bible does not endorse diversity, we can simply ignore the idea and focus on other essential issues for the church. However, if the Bible values the idea of diversity, we need to be all the more intentional about addressing the issue in the church. In what follows, we will examine whether diversity was part of God's intended design for his creation (Gen. 1–3), the church (Matt. 28:18–20; Acts 1:8; 6:1–7; 13:47–48; 16:9–10; 17:26–27; Gal. 3:28), and the future kingdom (Rev. 7:9). The content of the discussion will be crucial for laying a theological foundation for understanding faith formation in multiethnic contexts.

Diversity and God's Creation

The creation account recorded in Genesis 1–3 shows that diversity was clearly God's idea. A careful reading of the Genesis text suggests that diversity is tightly woven into the very fabric of creation, and human beings are part of it. The creation account indicates that God made a world of tremendous diversity when he created humans, animals, sea creatures, vegetation, planets, and all other creations. The wonders of God's creation affirm a diversity and a variety of things to the highest degree. God intentionally made this world diverse because he wills all things to work together in harmony for his good purpose. God's goodness is differentiated in various forms and shapes in all of his creation.

It is noteworthy that this created world reflects a clear statement regarding diversity in the Godhead. God's purpose in creating the world was to infuse his own diversity and tri-unity in the most suitable manner. Though this idea is foreign to some people, the word *Trinity* speaks of "threeness" within the Godhead. For instance, the Hebrew word for God used in Genesis 1:1 is *elohim* (אֱלֹהִים), the plural form of the word *el* (אֵל) (meaning God or deity). The plurality of God is also mentioned in Genesis 1:26. Notice the use of pronouns there. God said, "Let *us* make man in *our* image, after *our* likeness." To whom is God referring? If God is not three divine persons in one essence, the passage would not use plural first-person pronouns. There are other places in the book of Genesis where the plurality of the Godhead is also mentioned, such as in Genesis 3:22 after Adam and Eve sinned against God and also in Genesis 11:7, which is part of the story of the tower of Babel. A plurality within the Godhead is also explicitly taught in Matthew 3:16–17 (the baptism of Jesus), Matthew 28:19 (the Great Commission), 2 Corinthians 13:14 (Paul's benediction to the Corinthians), 1 Peter 1:2 (Peter's greeting to the Christians scattered in Asia Minor), and in many other places in the New Testament. All this is to say that, in essence, diversity stems from the triune God, who created humans as image bearers to reflect the diversity and unity of his nature, being one in essence yet subsisting in three distinct persons—the Father, the Son Jesus Christ, and the Holy Spirit (Luke 3:21–22; 1 Cor. 8:6; Eph. 4:1–6; Col. 1:15–17).

Diversity and God's Church

Whenever we think of the issue of diversity in the church, the story of Babel (Gen. 11:1–9)—God punishing prideful humanity with the curse of confusion and division—often comes to mind. Building on this story, some Christians argue that diversity is the result of humanity's rebellion against God, and they refuse to embrace ethnic and cultural diversity in the church. While God's action against the people of Babel brings the confusion of languages and the division of people (Gen. 11:7–8), we need to remember that Babel is not the end of the story.

At Pentecost (Acts 2), God reverses the curse of Babel and begins unifying people and nations. The tangible expression of this reversal is the commencement of the church—God's instrument for reuniting people who are separated by sin, culture, race, ethnicity, social class, and economics. As is clear from the book of Acts, the early church was made up of a diverse group of people. The ministry to make disciples of all nations (Matt. 28:18–20) commences with the coming of the Holy Spirit in Jerusalem (Acts 1–7) and then expands to Judea and Samaria (Acts 8–9) and to other parts of the world (Acts 10–28). As Christianity spread, the people of God, who started out as mostly Jewish believers, became a diverse international community.

As a result, the first multiethnic church was birthed in the city of Antioch (Acts 11:20). This is a powerful accomplishment of early Christians. During the first century, Antioch of Syria was a thriving Roman colony with a significant international population. This city was made up of eighteen different ethnic groups—Jews, Syrians, Arabs, Greeks, Persians, Armenians, Romans, Parthians, Cappadocians, Africans, and more.[4] Although diversity in the city caused conflict, division, riots, and low social capital among nonbelievers, Christ's followers rose above their racial and ethnic tensions and created a unified community filled with the grace and love of God (Acts 11:23). Due to this sacrificial effort, Antioch Christians were able to reverse the cultural alienation that existed in their society. Seeing every human as God's image bearer, these early believers ministered to a diverse group of people in the city and became a countercultural force in the first century (Gal. 2:11–14).

The grace of God destroyed the cultural and ethnic barriers and created a unified body of Christ made up of diverse people. What an amazing story!

Diversity and God's Kingdom

Just as creation and the church began with diversity in unity, so we will witness the rich diversity of humankind when the future kingdom of God is fully established. The kingdom story is consistent in its portrayal of an ethnically diverse future. The portrait of God's kingdom painted on the canvas of the Bible indicates that the kingdom to come will be ethnically more diverse than the typical racial and cultural homogeneity we observe in our local churches.

God's kingdom plan includes all nations of the earth (Gen. 18:18–19). While unity in Christ will still be the focus of the future kingdom, it will include a multitude of people who have various ethnic and cultural backgrounds (Rev. 5:9; 7:9–12). This intent to include all humanity is seen throughout the Bible. The first indicator is found in the Abrahamic covenant (Gen. 12:2–3; 17:4), or the so-called Old Testament mission mandate. With this mandate, God explains his plan to use the seed of Abraham to reach a multitude of nations (Gen. 17:4; Acts 3:25; Gal. 3:8). This plan was established in Genesis 12:2–3, renewed with Abraham's son and grandson (Gen. 26:2–5; 28:10–17), affirmed with the Israelites (Isa. 42:1–6; Jer. 31:31–37), formalized with the followers of Jesus Christ (Matt. 28:18–20; Luke 24:47; Eph. 4:11–12), and will be fully realized in the kingdom of God (Rev. 5:9; 7:9–12). Revelation 5:9 and 7:9–12 provide a portrait of the beauty of ethnic diversity in the future kingdom, where a great multitude of people from every nation, tribe, and language stands before God and worships him.

As can be gleaned from the discussion in the preceding paragraphs, diversity is intrinsic to our human existence, whether we are regenerated or not, because that is the way God created all people. For Christians, diversity is constitutive of a good spiritual community, since diversity stems from God, who created humans as image bearers to reflect his triune nature in the church and the world. That being said, unity in Christ is what all Christians should seek, especially in the pursuit of faith formation in the church. That is the will of God for all believers in Christ (John 17:23; Rom. 12:4; Eph. 1:10; 4:3, 13, 16).

Multiethnic Christian Faith

Building on the theoretical and theological insights of the previous sections, this section provides a conceptual framework for understanding the rational and relational dimensions of faith and their formative roles in the lives of multiethnic Christians. Theoretically speaking, the rational dimension represents the conscious commitment of the mind to biblical knowledge and belief, of which we have a clear understanding. The relational dimension represents faith-observant Christian practices or behaviors such as modes of prayer, expressions of spirituality, methods of spiritual discipline, forms of worship, and so on. In the multiethnic Christian life, the rational and relational dimensions of faith are inseparable. These dimensions interact with each other and cause faith to grow.

The discussion below explains what multiethnic faith is like, how it grows, and how it can take on certain cultural qualities despite its rootedness in evangelical Christian theology. The explanation is built on the premise that faith formation is an intricate process susceptible to various forms of scriptural and cultural influences. While faith in Jesus Christ is a work of God's grace toward believers (John 16:8; Rom. 3:22; 10:17; Eph. 2:8–9), it is experienced and developed secondarily within believers' ecclesio-cultural (i.e., church and cultural) context (John 17:15–19). This postulate reflects the two-dimensional nature of faith—that is, the rational and the relational—and binds faith formation with conceptual and experiential knowledge. Along with Scripture-informed conceptual knowledge, the way that multiethnic believers learn from ecclesio-cultural experiences becomes an important means to their faith formation. The rational and relational dimensions of faith and their roles in the multiethnic Christian life merit closer examination since they serve to clarify the premises and concepts essential for understanding the makeup and orientation of multiethnic faith.

The Didactic Connection between Scriptural Knowledge and the Rational Dimension of Multiethnic Christian Faith

The rational dimension of multiethnic faith represents the content domain of multiethnic faith being didactically connected to scriptural knowledge (see fig. 9.2). This inextricable connection produces a new heart in Christ, a regenerated form of spiritual consciousness, which orients a multiethnic believer to the self-Theos (God) nexus (Ps. 37:4; Jer. 24:7; Ezek. 11:19; 36:26; Rom. 12:2). This orientation of faith initiates an individual process of growing in the knowledge of God and causes multiethnic Christians to focus on the rational pursuit of faith. The Word of God, taught by the church and learned by individuals, forms the content in the rational dimension of multiethnic faith.

In order to comprehend the didactic connection between scriptural knowledge and the rational dimension of multiethnic faith, we need to

Figure 9.2
Multiethnic Christian faith

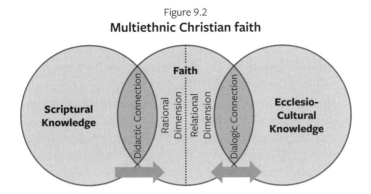

remember the three elements of faith that form its rational (or schematic) and relational (or thematic) dimensions. As asserted in chapter 3, faith has three elements: biblical knowledge, belief, and trust. Biblical knowledge and belief form the rational dimension of faith, and trust forms the relational dimension of faith. Because the inerrant Word of God shapes the knowledge and belief elements, the rational dimension is meta- and supra-cultural—that is, it stands above culture and can be applied in any context (Ps. 119:89; Isa. 40:8; Luke 16:17; John 8:32; 2 Tim. 3:16). However, the relational dimension can be subject to contextual influence and possess certain cultural qualities, since the trust element merely represents the practical outworking or behavioral output of faith situated in a believer's ecclesio-cultural context.

The theoretical scheme on the didactic connection is built on the contention that a unidirectional relationship exists between the rational dimension of multiethnic faith and scriptural knowledge, a form of conceptual knowledge enveloped in biblical principles (see fig. 9.2). The term *didactic* (from the Greek *didasko*, "to teach") refers to a pedagogy of teaching-learning involving facts and deduction. It conceptualizes multiethnic faith formation as an active process of comprehending the truth of God taught by the church and developing the content of faith. In the formation of multiethnic faith, the didactic connection implies the following pedagogical relationships: the teaching relationship between the multiethnic church and the congregation, and the learning relationship between Scripture and faith. In a broad sense, the teaching relationship refers to the ministry connection between the multiethnic church as a disciple maker and the congregation as a community of disciples. The learning relationship refers to the epistemic connection between the meaningfulness of scriptural content being learned and the growth of the congregation's faith.

Basically, the idea of didactic connection asserts that the pedagogical dynamic of teaching and learning is fundamentally rooted in multiethnic faith formation. The church becomes a didactician who provides learning opportunities and spiritual focus so that the congregation can learn meaningful biblical principles and grow in faith. In other words, multiethnic faith formation is linked to an ecclesial commitment to high-quality biblical teaching and a congregational commitment to learn and grow in the Word of God because the evidence of truth taught by the church produces proper knowledge, and the evidence of certainty learned by the congregation generates belief. The fusion of knowledge and belief becomes the cognitive source that forms the rational dimension of multiethnic faith. These cognitive sources of faith relate to "what a person knows and believes." Taken as a whole, multiethnic faith is built on a strong working knowledge of Scripture (John 8:32; 20:30–31; 1 Tim. 2:4; 2 Tim. 1:12).

The rational dimension is the backbone of multiethnic faith. Without the rational dimension guiding the formation process, multiethnic faith will not have any substance or vigor. While the relational dimension, discussed next, is an important component of multiethnic faith, it merely represents a by-product or behavior output of what multiethnic Christians know and believe in Christ.

The Dialogic Connection between Ecclesio-cultural Knowledge and the Relational Dimension of Multiethnic Christian Faith

The relational dimension of multiethnic faith represents the behavioral domain of multiethnic faith being dialogically connected to ecclesio-cultural knowledge (see fig. 9.2). This dynamic connection produces collective empathy, a Christian form of sociocultural consciousness, which orients multiethnic Christians to the self-others nexus. This orientation of faith allows multiethnic Christians to regard faith as part of a larger and more inclusive whole in the spiritual life. Drawing upon the communal spiritual heritage of the church and the spiritual needs of others, multiethnic Christians learn to approach faith as the gift of God that is to be received together with other believers in the church, similar to how the early Christians understood the communal value of faith (Acts 2:42, 47; 1 Cor. 10:24; Eph. 4:12–16).

In order to comprehend the dialogic connection mentioned above, we need to understand what collective empathy is and how it functions in the lives of multiethnic Christians. Collective empathy is a keen awareness embedded in the worldview of multiethnic Christians. It operates as a potent suggestion and assists multiethnic Christians to externalize their faith to maintain harmony with other believers. As opposed to cognitive empathy, collective empathy denotes how an individual's empathic emotion emerges to become more group oriented. It stems from intergroup emotions theory,[5] which explains the relationship between human emotions and social groups. The theory assumes that since the group is incorporated in the collective self, the stronger one's association with the group, the more likely the person will experience group-based emotions. This is especially true for multiethnic Christians. Since they are exposed to a diverse group of people, they naturally develop a more inclusive and accommodating kind of mindfulness, which becomes a cognitive basis for recognizing and embracing the state of difference with others. This shared understanding of others grows and develops into sociocultural consciousness as collective empathy. In the life of multiethnic faith, collective empathy functions as the epistemic basis of ecclesio-cultural knowledge.

The theoretical scheme on the dialogic connection is built on the contention that a reciprocal relationship exists between the relational dimension of multiethnic faith and ecclesio-cultural knowledge, a form of experiential knowledge enveloped by collective empathy (see fig. 9.2). The term *dialogue* (Gk. *dialogos*, from *dia*, "through, across," and *logos*, "word, opinion, reason, speech") refers to a form of integrative knowing involving experience and induction. The idea of dialogue conceptualizes multiethnic faith formation as a continuous process of apprehending knowledge from ecclesio-cultural experience and developing the structure of faith. For example, when multiethnic Christians engage in the life of faith, they must cautiously negotiate with others surrounding their spiritual life. The ecclesio-cultural community, which they are a part of, expects them to cautiously accommodate the community's spiritual and sociocultural expectations. Subsequently, multiethnic Christians learn to dialogically adjust their relational dimension of faith to fit the expectations of the community while maintaining their rational focus on the Bible. For this reason, many multiethnic Christians are able to develop a culturally engaging yet theologically conservative evangelical faith. Their knowledge of ecclesio-cultural context and Scripture becomes a catalyst for forming this type of holistic faith.

When studying faith formation among multiethnic Christians, we need to remember the role that the relational dimension of faith plays in their lives. Although faith is born of an individual encounter with the living God through Jesus Christ, it can take on context-specific textures and expressions due to ecclesio-cultural influences. Various beliefs and practices embedded in a local ecclesio-cultural community become a potent source of this type of influence. The multiethnic Christian life is not an individual affair devoid of cultural influence.

Conclusion

As was indicated at the outset of this chapter, it is important to understand faith formation in multiethnic contexts. In the formation of faith among multiethnic Christians, the rational dimension represents a doctrinal character of faith—namely, what they know and believe in Christ. The relational dimension represents a functional character of faith—namely, how they live out their trust in life. It is through maintaining a delicate balance between these two dimensions of faith that multiethnic Christians are able to grow in congruence with their biblical and cultural DNA.

Discussion Questions

1. What is culture? What relationship exists between faith and culture?
2. Is the idea of cultural diversity biblical or unbiblical? Please explain your answer.
3. Does culture influence faith? If yes, how does culture affect the way we understand and grow in faith? If no, why not?
4. Does faith influence culture? If yes, how does faith influence the way we view and approach culture? If no, why not?
5. Explain the difference between multiethnicity and multiculturalism. How should Christians respond to these theories of cultural diversity?
6. Explain the difference between assimilation and acculturation. How should Christians respond to these theories of cultural adaptation?
7. How would you explain the relationship between the rational dimension and the relational dimension of faith discussed in this chapter?
8. How can local churches become more effective at educating their members in biblical faith?

Further Reading

DeYmaz, Mark, and Bob Whitesel. *re:MIX: Transitioning Your Church to Living Color*. Nashville: Abingdon, 2016.

DeYmaz, Mark, and George Yancey. *Building a Healthy Multi-Ethnic Church: Mandate, Commitments, and Practices of a Diverse Congregation*. San Francisco: Jossey-Bass, 2007.

Hiebert, Paul. *Transforming Worldviews: An Anthropological Understanding of How People Change*. Grand Rapids: Baker Academic, 2008.

Kullberg, Kelly Monroe, and Lael Arrington. *Faith and Culture: A Guide to a Culture Shaped by Faith*. Grand Rapids: Zondervan, 2011.

McIntosh, Gary, and Alan McMahan. *Being the Church in a Multi-Ethnic Community: Why It Matters and How It Works*. Fishers, IN: Wesleyan Publishing, 2012.

10

Faith Formation in Global Contexts

The wind of change is blowing through the church. It was not too long ago that the church witnessed the emergence of fundamental Christianity, concerned with combating theological and cultural liberalism (from the late 1800s to the early 1900s), and the movement of evangelical Christianity, concerned with defending the doctrine of justification through faith in Jesus Christ (from the 1950s to the present). Today in the church, there is a movement of global Christianity that seeks to uphold the Christian faith within a rapidly changing world.

As the transcontinental flows of people, culture, and ideas are reshaping the church worldwide, Christian leaders are in the midst of an unprecedented conversation about globalization. While some leaders are contesting globalization, many leaders view it as an inevitable and irreversible trend that needs to be studied in the church. They attempt to lay out extensive analyses of globalization and seek to understand the relationship between transnational culture and the Christian faith. Globalization has brought Christianity into a new era.

The aim of this chapter is to present a well-defined conceptual framework of global faith formation. Several key terms will be used throughout the discussion. The term *faith* will be used synonymously with the Christian faith. The terms *global faith* and *diasporic faith* will be synonymous with global Christian faith and diasporic Christian faith, respectively.

Globalization and Culture

Globalization in its simplistic sense represents the face of the world today. People live in a global age of deep diversity and heightened complexity. Observers of this movement have paid attention to the worldwide sociocultural, economic, political, and religious changes and their implications for nations, governments, corporations, and churches.

In a nutshell, the concept of globalization has physical and ideological dimensions. The physical dimension of globalization represents an international expansion of human activities across different parts of the world and a movement toward a single world structure. The proliferation of technological innovations (such as the internet, television, mobile technology, and the Internet of Things), the growth of human travel, and the expansion of Christianity have contributed significantly to this physical movement of globalization. The ideological dimension involves the development of transnational and transcultural self-consciousness that links human minds across great stretches of cultures and societies. This cognitive component of globalization is part of an ever-growing relationship that is characterized by the voluntary exchange and reciprocal absorption of cultural ideas.

In the study of globalization, cultural globalization describes a multidimensional phenomenon involving worldwide interactions that lead to transnational interconnectivity and interdependence among various people groups. In a simplistic sense, cultural globalization entails the deepening of sociocultural interconnectivity and interdependence of people located on a continuum of the regional and the continental. At one end of the continuum is social interconnectivity that joins and expands human interactions around the world. This means simply that everything that happens locally affects everyone globally. At the other end is a cultural interdependence that allows people and organizations to share various ideas, goods, and resources together. In general, cultural globalization in the twenty-first century is about people becoming increasingly united and dependent on one another. Physical distances are no longer important. What happens in one place affects people elsewhere.

As members of the global community, we need to ask the following question: As the world becomes increasingly borderless, does cultural globalization lead to the homogenization of culture, to the heterogenization of culture, or to the hybridization of culture? Cultural homogenization is an assimilation process taking place at the transnational level. It simply means that local cultures are *absorbed* into a dominant culture. As a result, cultural homogenization decreases cultural diversity and results in a single global culture. Cultural heterogenization, which is also called glocalization, is an acculturation process taking place at the transnational level. It is about *adopting* various values, beliefs, and systems of other cultures while preserving one's local culture. Cultural heterogenization increases cultural diversity and leads to a multicultural world. Cultural hybridization, on the other hand, concocts different cultural beliefs, values, symbols, and practices to create something that is new and meaningful to participants. This process involves synthesizing elements of various cultures and creating a new transnational culture. While it is difficult to answer the question raised above, it is safe to assume that on the surface level, the hybridization of culture naturally accompanies globalization.

To do proper ministry in the twenty-first century, every believer needs to study how globalization accompanied by cultural hybridization affects the Christian life and to acquire the proper skills necessary for global ministry. Christians can no longer exist in the world as individualized, monocultural beings apart from others. Everyone is interconnected in the global body of Jesus Christ.

Globalization and Christianity

Christianity as a Global Faith

Christianity is a global faith. The Christian faith has always been global in the sense that it was established as a gospel mission to reach the world for Jesus Christ (Matt. 28:18–20; Mark 16:15; John 20:21–23; Acts 1:4–8). While maintaining its solid core on the uncompromising Word of God, it sought to maintain soft, permeable edges to attract the lost to the Christian faith. From the beginning, this faith was founded on the sharing of the good news that is rooted in the mission of Christ.

With the Great Commission, the last recorded personal instruction given by Jesus to his disciples and to all his future followers, Christianity spread. In the first four centuries of the church, Christianity spread slowly but steadily throughout the Roman Empire. After Emperor Constantine issued the Edict of Milan (AD 313), which established Christianity as the official religion of the Roman Empire, Christianity spread rapidly in the Greco-Roman world, including India (first century) and Central Asia (second century). Following the fall of the Roman Empire (AD 476), Christianity spread throughout northern Europe, then to China (seventh century) and Russia (ninth to tenth centuries). During the medieval period, it spread to East Asia (seventh to thirteenth centuries) and Southeast Asia (twelfth to sixteenth centuries). Although the negative forces of classical antiquity, humanism, modernism, and postmodernism sought to dismantle the movement of Christianity, it continued to expand globally. Today, Christianity has more adherents than any other religious group. What was once considered a religious movement of the Mediterranean world has become a religion of the world. Currently, one-third of all humans, about 33 percent of the world's population, is Christian.[1] Christianity has become a global faith.

The Shifting Center of Global Christianity

Although the overall Christian population is still growing in the twenty-first century, its increase is mainly coming from the global South. The main growth is significant in the geographical regions of Africa, Asia, and Latin America. In the early 1900s, Christianity was considered the religion of the global North, such as Europe and North America. Over 80 percent of the world's Christians lived in the global North. However, this figure had dropped to 43 percent by 1970. It is estimated that over 66 percent of all Christians will come from the global South in the near future.[2]

With the decline of the Christian population in the global North, Christianity's center of gravity has shifted to the global South. The vibrant growth of churches in Africa, the explosion of evangelical churches in Asia, and the rise of Pentecostal churches in Latin America are dramatically changing the demographic landscape of Christianity worldwide.[3] One interesting fact associated with this phenomenon is that more and more Christian missionaries are coming from the global South. This means that reverse missions are taking place. Traditionally, missionaries were sent mainly from Europe and North America to southern nations. Now missionaries from former mission fields are bringing the gospel back to northern nations. The global South has become the epicenter of Christianity.

The southern shift in Christianity is not only changing the landscape of Christian demographics but also transforming the way we understand faith. The rapid growth of Christianity around the globe has brought new perspectives and new expressions to the way the faith is understood and lived out. In particular, Christians from Africa, Asia, and Latin America are seeking to understand faith formation with their collectivist worldview and to contextualize faith in a culturally relevant yet redemptive way in their contexts. For church ministry and the Christian life, they are imposing a greater need for cultural relevance on faith.

Globalization and the Diaspora Church

Diaspora Christians

Adding to the global spread of the Christian faith is the development of the diaspora church, which made major inroads into the global Christian landscape and is contributing much to the movement of the gospel in the world. It is estimated that 859 million people from 327 people groups live in diaspora. This estimation is staggering because it indicates that 12.5 percent of the world population (or a little more than one out of ten people) is living abroad or on the move. Of this diaspora population, Christians make up the largest share. It is estimated that nearly half (47.4 percent) of diasporas are Christians,[4] about 407 million people or 5.9 percent of the world population.

Diaspora Christians are contributing much to the global expansion and revitalization of the Christian faith. They bring faith with them wherever they go, planting churches and getting involved in local community evangelism. One of their primary concerns is to establish the local church as a redeemed community for kingdom work (Matt. 6:10; 28:18–20; Luke 22:29; Acts 2:42–47; Col. 1:13–14; Heb. 10:24–25; Rev. 1:6). Global demographic trends estimate that the number of diaspora Christians will continually increase over the next few decades, and they will have a profound impact on the future of the Christian faith. Diaspora Christians have become major players in the expansion of the Christian faith in the world.

Biblical Meaning of Diaspora

The studies of diasporas in missiological circles mainly focus on contemporary migrant Christian communities in the world, drawing attention to their growing number and their cultural-religious characteristics. While the concept of diaspora has become a buzzword in the discourse on global missions and has caused widespread discussions and debates, little attention has been given to its biblical meaning.

The term *diaspora* is a biblical concept that has its origin in ancient Jewish history. *Diaspora* (διασπορά) is a transliteration of a Greek feminine noun that means "dispersion." It is a derivative of the verb *diaspeirō* (διασπείρω), which means "to scatter abroad" or "to be dispersed." The biblical use of *diaspora*, as exemplified in the Septuagint (Deut. 28:25; Ps. 146:2; Isa. 49:6; Jer. 15:7) and in the New Testament (John 7:35; James 1:1), stems from the Hebrew word for exile (Heb. גָּלוּת, *galut*), which refers to the historic dispersion of the Jews.

In the Old Testament and in other ancient Jewish literature, *diaspora* was used to describe the dispersion and the widespread settlement of Israelites outside their homeland. In the first instance, the term was used in reference to the dispersion of ethnic Jews from Israel to a foreign land (Deut. 28:25; 30:4; Isa. 49:6; Jer. 15:7; 41:17). The first Jewish diaspora happened when the Assyrian Empire deported the Northern Kingdom of Israel in the eighth century BC. However, the more permanent Jewish diaspora took place during the Babylonia exile in the sixth century BC, when Nebuchadnezzar forcefully relocated Jews from the Southern Kingdom of Judah to Babylon. Another well-known dispersion of Jews took place during the Hellenistic and Roman periods (fourth century BC to fifth century AD). As a result, Jewish diasporic communities were formed in North Africa and across the Mediterranean world (James 1:1; 1 Pet. 1:1). The major concern for these Jewish diasporas was maintaining harmony between the cultures and customs of their home country and those of their host country. While plunging themselves into the memories of the past, they sought to adjust to new cultural environments.

While the term *diaspora* was a historical descriptor for the Jewish dispersion outside their homeland, it became a figurative expression for Christians' status as sojourners and pilgrims in the world. The Bible declares that all Christians are diasporas who are placed around the world for kingdom work (Matt. 24:14; 28:19; Mark 13:27; 16:15; Luke 3:6; 24:47; Acts 1:8; 3:25; Rom. 14:11; Gal. 3:8; Rev. 7:9; 14:6). Just as early Christians who fled Jerusalem ended up spreading the gospel in the provinces of Asia Minor (Eph. 2:19; 1 Pet. 1:1; 2:11), contemporary diaspora Christians are spreading the gospel as they move from one country to another. Theologically speaking, the diaspora movement represents God's sovereign act of relocating his people around the world for the work of the gospel.

Sociological Meanings of Diaspora

While the concept of diaspora derives its meaning from the Bible, it has acquired renewed importance in academic discussions. In the field of intercultural studies in particular, it has become a theoretical construct with wider applications. The body of literature in intercultural studies distinguishes diaspora as a sociological category. It explains diaspora as a sociocultural manifestation of migrant communities.

Until the 1990s, the use of the term *diaspora* in Christian literature was mostly connected to the negative ideas of rebellion, exile, and homelessness. The use of the term was often linked to the Jews who were forcibly dispersed into foreign lands because they had discarded the righteous pathway toward relationship with God. The concept of diaspora implied the devastating impetus for and outcome of God's judgment. However, this negative meaning is virtually lost in contemporary discussions of diaspora. The modern use of the term has widened to include migrant transnational communities scattered around the world for various reasons, including but not limited to business, education, missions, immigration, military service, political conflict, and religious persecution. At present, diaspora in public discourse refers to transnational communities formed by global migrations and transcultural activities.

Contemporary studies of diaspora no longer confine the term to the physical relocation of migrants. Diaspora now denotes ideological repositioning and reformulation. It implies a transnational or global consciousness that has a hybrid form of beliefs, values, and meanings accommodated from intercultural encounters and adaptations. It represents a hybrid form of transethnic, translingual, and transcultural consciousness.

Faith Formation in Global Contexts: A Diasporic Christian View

The study of faith formation in the twenty-first century leads to the issue of faith and transnational culture. As the church of Jesus Christ becomes universal, the question of the interrelationship of faith and transnational culture becomes all the more important in church ministry. The dramatic changes brought forth by global church movements are not only bringing new ecclesial challenges but also raising deep questions about the way we understand the relationship between faith and culture.

This section will develop a conceptual framework for understanding faith formation in global contexts. To do this, we will consider a formation pattern of diasporic faith as a basic framework to study how the ministries of education and edification offered in the diaspora church create a theological space conducive to formal nurture of faith and how the vertical and horizontal dimensions of fellowship (*koinonia*) embedded in the diaspora church create a relational space conducive for the informal nurture of faith (see fig. 10.1). *Space* as a trope denotes the pedagogy's balance of attending to the spiritual and personal needs of the diaspora church's members and providing a holistic ministry that is biblically faithful and culturally relevant.

Figure 10.1
Diasporic Model of Faith Formation

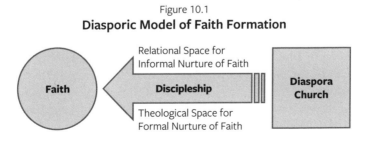

Relational Space for Informal Nurture of Faith

Faith

Discipleship

Diaspora Church

Theological Space for Formal Nurture of Faith

Theological Space of the Diaspora Church

The theological space represents the formal ministry environment created by the ministries of education and edification. Despite the overwhelming challenges that globalization brings to ministry, the diaspora church is committed to educating and edifying its members for ministry—the principal tasks of discipleship (Matt. 28:18–20; Eph. 3:17–19; Col. 2:6–7; Heb. 6:1–2; 2 Pet. 3:18). These tasks create a formal learning environment conducive for biblical faith formation. Pedagogically, a formal discipleship environment is called a theological space. The concept of formal space here represents a transformative learning environment where church members are able to learn, reflect, and integrate biblical truth with their faith. The formal knowledge of the Bible learned in the theological space becomes one of the two critical strands that are interwoven into diasporic faith (see fig. 10.1).

Inner Dimension of Theological Space and Diasporic Faith

The inner dimension of theological space in the diaspora church is created by the ministry of education. The ministry of education represents the diaspora church's effort to strengthen believers' minds with the truth of God. Diaspora church leaders are increasingly aware that improving the quality of ministry largely depends on creating a transformative learning space where their members are able to learn, reflect, and integrate biblical truth with their faith. So the church is intentional about creating a formal learning environment where the transformative nature of knowing can take root in members' faith.

In keeping with the Protestant Christian heritage, diaspora church leaders believe that the church is God's perfected agent assigned to convey the knowledge of God in this world and to educate its members for the work of the gospel (Matt. 16:18; Eph. 2:10; 1 Pet. 2:9). Therefore, the church does not exclude formal teaching. The church orchestrates its efforts to teach theological knowledge by preaching exegetical sermons, providing opportunities for Bible studies, and introducing laypeople to methods of hermeneutics. The church is committed to biblical teaching because the content of the Bible informs faith and cultivates Christlikeness. While the major trend of ministry in the West focuses more on the learner-centered epistemology of knowing, in which meaning and relevance are emphasized in teaching, the leaders of the diaspora church are committed to the subject-centered epistemology of knowing, in which content, meaning, and application are emphasized in teaching. It is through participating in this type of formal learning that diaspora Christians are able to grow in the knowledge of God and to form biblically sound faith in Christ (1 Cor. 13:2; Phil. 1:9–11; 2 Pet. 3:18).

Theologically rich and Scripture-saturated education contributes to the development of diasporic faith. Although faith formation can never be reduced to formal learning of the Bible, if formal learning is accompanied by informal learning, faith will have its proper balance.

Outer Dimension of Theological Space and Diasporic Faith

The outer dimension of theological space in the diaspora church is created by the ministry of edification. The ministry of edification represents the diaspora church's effort to build up its members and help them engage the world with the gospel of Jesus Christ. The church's ministry of edification consists of two foundational elements: leadership training and missional engagement. As explicitly commanded in the Bible, the diaspora church utilizes lay leadership and missions training as the means to strengthen members' faith and to prepare them for the work of ministry in the world (Matt. 28:18–20; Eph. 4:11–13).

To accomplish the church's formational task, the diaspora church provides lay leadership training at both individual and community levels. At the individual level, diaspora lay leadership training is designed to nurture members' spiritual relationship with God. The diaspora church is committed to the ordinary means of lay spiritual training, guiding members into a deeper faith in God and helping them to develop Christlike character. Church leaders believe that as their training engages the minds of believers, the Holy Spirit will transform members' hearts and behaviors in the power of Christ. And the outcome is transformed faith. At the community level, diaspora lay leadership training is designed to nurture members to serve the church. The church equips and empowers members to take on various ministry responsibilities. The diaspora church firmly believes that one of the best ways to grow faith is by serving. Christian service promotes and ignites passion for Christ and vitalizes faith.

To accomplish the church's missional task, diaspora church leaders direct their ministry toward preparing every member for the work of missions. Missions training within the diasporic church is a multidimensional process that takes place as a result of integrating theological and cultural principles. While maintaining a conservative stance on evangelical theology, members are taught to contextualize the key elements of the gospel that are relevant to sharing their faith in various cultural contexts. The training, which includes local community outreach and short-term mission opportunities, helps members to orient their faith toward the world.

The diaspora church fully embraces the principal tasks of educating and edifying its members so they can grow in biblical faith. Despite immense cultural challenges, the diaspora church is still committed to teaching distinctives of biblical faith to its members and equipping them to grow as disciples of Jesus Christ. The ministries of education and edification represent a practical expression of the diaspora church's mission—the role that it takes on as a disciple-making community in transnational contexts.

Relational Space of the Diaspora Church

The relational space represents the informal ministry environment created by the vertical and horizontal dimensions of *koinonia* (Gk. κοινωνία, "fellowship"). Vertical *koinonia* is the deep, personal communion that believers have with God. Horizontal *koinonia* is the interpersonal communion that believers have with one another. Along with the formal ministries of education and edification, the diaspora church utilizes ecclesial fellowship as an informal way to nurture members' faith.

Pedagogically, this informal ministry environment is called a relational space. The concept of relational space here represents a transformative learning environment that encourages members to informally learn, reflect on, and integrate biblical truth with their faith as they commune with God and other believers. Among diaspora Christians, the informal knowledge learned in ecclesial fellowship is the other critical strand that is interwoven into their faith (see fig. 10.1).

Vertical *Koinonia* and Diasporic Faith

Diasporic faith formation is a personal process that involves vertical *koinonia*. The diaspora church believes that all human beings are given the capacity for spiritual relatedness, so having intimate communion with the triune God becomes foremost a matter of ontological necessity for believers' faith growth. The ideas of one God existing in a Trinity of persons (*perichoresis*, περιχώρησις) and the three persons sharing the life of one another (*koinonia*, κοινωνία) become the intricate base for faith formation. The terms *perichoresis* and *koinonia* indicate the ideas of circumincession (or reciprocal existence) and communion, respectively. In an effort to apply these doctrinal concepts in ministry, the church encourages members to become actively involved in an individual walk with God and teaches them to make their best effort to grow first at the personal level. Particular emphasis is placed on embracing deep, spiritual fellowship with God so that the circumincession and communion of the Trinity reflected in vertical *koinonia* can create a natural atmosphere for faith growth.

Educationally speaking, vertical *koinonia* represents a hidden curriculum of the diaspora church. This vertical dimension of ecclesial fellowship creates an atmosphere for informal learning and serves to reinforce the formal learning obtained from the ministries of education and edification. A hidden curriculum is the implicit and unstructured learning that occurs through the experience of participating in individual communion. It refers to a type of learning that is caught rather than taught. Vertical *koinonia* creates a sense of connection and relatedness to God and solidifies the faith of diaspora Christians.

As can be gleaned from the discussion above, the Trinity is the basic framework for understanding the connection between vertical *koinonia* and diasporic faith. A trinitarian understanding of God not only paints a picture of God in communion with the other members of the Trinity but also teaches us about the God who is in communion with us and transforming our faith. It reminds Christians of the value and significance of having a personal walk with God in the entire process of faith formation. As a matter of fact, the Bible teaches that vertical *koinonia* and faith are closely connected and that it was the personal connection with the triune God that allowed early Christians to share everything they had with other believers (Acts 2:42–47; 1 Cor. 11:24–26).

God is a relational being who exists in deep communion and invites all believers to commune with him personally. When believers participate in vertical *koinonia*, the three divine persons of the Trinity are actively involved in the entire scheme of spiritual life and cause faith to grow. Participating in the divine trinitarian life through intimate communion is foundational to diasporic faith.

Horizontal *Koinonia* and Diasporic Faith

Diasporic faith formation is also a communal process that involves horizontal *koinonia*. Diaspora church leaders are questing for holistic nurture of faith because they believe that the triune God has given one faith to be celebrated among diverse groups of believers (Matt. 28:19; 2 Cor. 1:21–22; 13:14; Gal. 3:28; Eph. 4:5; Rev. 7:9–10). In the same way that each person of the Trinity possesses the common essence and nature of the Trinity in his own way while being united to the other persons, being a Christian does not mean a loss of individual particularity but rather an enhancing of a person's individual and cultural qualities. So the church encourages members to love one other and to respect one another's cultural heritage.

In the diaspora church, the relational space entailed in ecclesial fellowship naturally creates an atmosphere for informal learning and causes members to grow with a Christian form of transnational consciousness—a form of global awareness that is attained through the hybridized selection of two or more cultures during the enculturation process. This type of consciousness produces an awareness of the interconnectivity of people across cultural boundaries. As a cognitive framework, transnational consciousness represents a legitimate form of knowledge developed from the intercultural encounter of others. It is a mental framework that is shaped by diverse cultural beliefs, values, traditions, and practices. It can be dual or multiple in makeup and is formed by the ideological dissonance and integration involving a complex mixture of sociocultural and historical conditions created during intercultural encounters. The rest of this section uses the term *global Christian consciousness* (GCC) to describe a Christian form of transnational consciousness. In the life of diasporic faith, GCC serves as a key agent that forms the global character and content of diasporic faith.

GCC represents a transnational mindset of diaspora Christians. As an ideological category, GCC represents a hybridized worldview constructed from the Christ-centered encounter of various cultural beliefs, values, and traditions. GCC is dialectically configured from ideological assimilation and accommodation of two or more cultural worldviews. The boundaries of social space in a new cultural setting cause diaspora Christians to assimilate and accommodate perplexing experiences, issues, and thoughts into their lives. Such an awareness initially produces an inner tension when a person encounters a new culture, but it eventually brings cognitive harmony by modifying existing beliefs and assimilating the new awareness of culture synchronically. This process of hybridization is quite intricate and involves theological reflection and critical assessment of the various metaphysical, epistemological, and axiological principles embedded in cultures.

In the diasporic Christian life, GCC expands the horizon of faith beyond the homogeneous singularity of monoculturalism and toward the heterogeneous expressivity of transnationalism. Such an awareness creates a faith stance that is global and kingdom focused. And this type of intercultural experience allows Christians to generate a more inclusive type of faith that values others before the self (Matt. 22:39). For example, third-culture Christians also own this type of global Christian consciousness.[5] A third culture is a by-product of globalization and refers to a reinvented, reconstructed, and reestablished set of values, beliefs, and norms based on the hybridization of two or more worldviews. A third culture is often owned by expatriates, especially their children, who learn to create and live in an interstitial sociocultural space between a native culture of their parents and a host culture of the country in which they live. The hybridization process of third culture is not about simply combining different elements of cultures together; merely fusing cultures would generate muddled and characterless consciousness as a whole. The developing third culture involves integrating the various beliefs, values, and traditions encountered in life and dialectically constructing a new consciousness based on a Christian worldview.

One of the principal objectives for presenting a diasporic framework of faith formation in this section is to draw attention to the dynamic connection that exists between the global Christian faith, theological training, and ecclesial fellowship. The idea of dynamicity denotes a critical process by which theological training grounds faith to its rational root. And the idea of connectivity denotes a reflective process by which ecclesial fellowship grounds faith to its relational root. It is due to this dynamic connection that diaspora Christians are able to grow in wholesome faith.

Conclusion

The Christian faith is a global faith. As the Christian community becomes increasingly diverse and globalized, the church needs to increase its understanding of transnational culture, particularly as it relates to the faith and life of its congregations. By having a proper knowledge of transnational culture, the church can offer holistic ministry to its members. Furthermore, having such knowledge will also be important as the church looks toward the future kingdom, where people from diverse cultures will come together, worshiping God and living in harmony (Rom. 15:8–13; Rev. 7:9–17).

Discussion Questions

1. What is globalization? What are the benefits and drawbacks of globalization?
2. How does globalization impact culture? Has the cultural form of globalization gone too far or not far enough?
3. What does it mean to be Christians in the global era? Do we need to adapt to or reject the changes taking place around the globe?
4. Has globalization had any effects on you and your family? What practical challenges and conflicts do you or your family face? In what ways?
5. What influence does the globalization of culture have on your Christian life, church ministry, and missions?
6. What is the relationship between faith and transnational culture?

| Further Reading

Bradshaw, Bruce. *Changes across Cultures*. Grand Rapids: Baker Academic, 2012.

Elmer, Duane. *Cross-Cultural Connections: Stepping Out and Fitting In around the World*. Downers Grove, IL: InterVarsity, 2002.

Hiebert, Paul G., and Eloise Meneses Hiebert. *Incarnational Ministry: Planting Churches in Band, Tribal, Peasant, and Urban Societies*. Grand Rapids: Baker, 1995.

Im, Chandler H., and Amos Yong. *Global Diasporas and Mission*. Oxford: Regnum Books, 2014.

Johnson, Todd M. *Christianity in Its Global Context, 1970–2020: Society, Religion, and Mission*. South Hamilton, MA: Gordon-Conwell Theological Seminary Center for the Study of Global Christianity, 2013.

Johnstone, Patrick. *The Future of the Global Church: History, Trends and Possibilities*. Downers Grove, IL: InterVarsity, 2014.

Plueddemann, James. *Leading across Cultures: Effective Ministry and Mission in the Global Church*. Downers Grove, IL: InterVarsity, 2009.

Notes

Chapter 1: Faith Formation in the Bible

1. W. E. Vines, "Believe," in *Expository Dictionary of Biblical Words*, ed. W. E. Vine, Merrill F. Unger, and William White (Nashville: Thomas Nelson, 1985), 116–17.

2. Rudolf Bultmann and Artur Weiser, "πιστεύω κτλ," in *Theological Dictionary of the New Testament*, vol. 6, ed. Gerhard Kittel and Gerhard Friedrich (Grand Rapids: Eerdmans, 1968), 182–83.

3. Joseph P. Healey, "Faith: Old Testament," in *Anchor Bible Dictionary*, vol. 2, ed. David Noel Freedman (New York: Doubleday, 1992), 745.

4. Jack B. Scott, "*ĕmûnâ*," *Theological Wordbook of the Old Testament*, vol. 1, ed. R. Laird Harris, Gleason L. Archer Jr., and Bruce K. Waltke (Chicago: Moody, 1980), 52.

5. Dieter Lührmann, "Faith: New Testament," in Freedman, *Anchor Bible Dictionary*, 2:750–51.

6. O. Michel, "NT *pistis*," in *The New International Dictionary of New Testament Theology*, vol. 1, ed. Colin Brown (Grand Rapids: Zondervan, 1975), 599–605.

7. Cf. W. E. Vines, "Belief, Believe, Believers," in *Expository Dictionary of New Testament Terms* (Old Tappan, NJ: Revell, 1971), 116–17.

8. W. E. Vines, "Faith," in Vine, Unger, and White, *Expository Dictionary of Biblical Words*, 71.

9. Handley Dunelm, "Faith," in *International Standard Bible Encyclopedia*, vol. 2 (Grand Rapids: Eerdmans, 1939), 1088.

10. Cf. Dennis R. Lindsay, "Believing in Jesus: John's Provocative Theology of Faith," *Restoration Quarterly* 58, no. 4 (2016): 193–209.

11. Gregg R. Allison, "Salvation and Christian Education," in *A Theology for Christian Education*, ed. James Riley Estep Jr., Gregg R. Allison, and Michael J. Anthony (Nashville: B&H, 2008), 227. Cf. also Klaus Issler, "Faith," in *Evangelical Dictionary of Christian Education*, ed. Michael J. Anthony, Warren Benson, Daryl Eldridge, and Julie Gorman (Grand Rapids: Baker Academic, 2001), 283–85.

12. Healey, "Faith: Old Testament," in *Anchor Bible Dictionary*, 2:744–49.

13. Cf. Perry Downs, "Faith Development," in Anthony et al., *Evangelical Dictionary of Christian Education*, 285–88.

14. James E. Loder, *The Transforming Moment* (Colorado Springs: Helmers & Howard, 1989).

15. L. L. Morris, "Faith," in *Illustrated Bible Dictionary*, vol. 1 (Nashville: Tyndale, 1986), 496.

16. J. I. Packer, "Faith," in *Evangelical Dictionary of Theology*, 3rd ed., ed. Daniel J. Treier and Walter A. Elwell (Grand Rapids: Baker Academic, 2017), 303.

17. Louis Berkhof, *Systematic Theology* (Grand Rapids: Eerdmans, 1941), 494–95.

18. Craig R. Dykstra, "Faith," in *Encyclopedia of Religious Education* (New York: Harper & Row, 1990), 245–46.

19. Packer, "Faith," 303. This would parallel the process of affective learning explained in James Riley Estep, "Childhood Transformation: Toward an Educational Theology of Childhood Conversion and Spiritual Formation," *Stone-Campbell Journal* 5, no. 2 (2002): 183–206.

20. Caspar Wistar Hodge, "Faithful, Faithfulness," in *International Standard Bible Encyclopedia*, vol. 2 (Grand Rapids: Eerdmans, 1939), 1088–91.

21. This is the title of his insightful work on discipleship, published by InterVarsity in 2000.

22. D. A. Carson, *Gagging of God* (Grand Rapids: Zondervan, 1996), 555–56.

23. See Leon J. Wood, *The Holy Spirit in the Old Testament* (Grand Rapids: Zondervan, 1981).

24. Issler, "Faith," 285.

Chapter 2: Faith Formation in the Christian Tradition

1. Karen Swallow Prior, *On Reading Well* (Grand Rapids: Brazos, 2018), 107.

2. Frederick Christian Bauerschmidt and James J. Buckley, *Catholic Theology: An Introduction* (Malden, MA: Wiley & Sons, 2017), 335–39.

3. Frederick Christian Bauerschmidt, *Thomas Aquinas: Faith, Reason, and Following Christ* (Oxford: Oxford University Press, 2013), 145.

4. Geoffrey W. Bromiley, *Historical Theology: An Introduction* (Grand Rapids: Eerdmans, 1978), 230–37; Justo L. González, *A History of Christian Thought*, vol. 3 (Nashville: Abingdon, 1975), 50–51.

5. Ewald M. Plass, *What Luther Says: An Anthology*, vol. 1 (St. Louis: Concordia, 1959), 466.

6. Plass, *What Luther Says*, 466.

7. John Calvin, *Commentary on St. Paul's Epistle to the Galatians and Ephesians* (Grand Rapids: Eerdmans, 1957), comments on Ephesians 2:8.

8. Louis Berkhof, *Systematic Theology* (Grand Rapids: Eerdmans, 1941), 497.

9. Richard A. Muller, "The Priority of the Intellect in the Soteriology of Jacob Arminius," *Wesleyan Theological Journal* 55 (1993): 55–72.

10. Susan F. Harrington, "Friendship Under Fire: George Whitefield and John Wesley, 1739–1741," *Andover Newton Quarterly* 15, no. 3 (1975): 167–81.

11. James L. Schwenk, *Catholic Spirit: Wesley, Whitefield, and the Quest for Evangelical Unity in Eighteenth-Century British Methodism* (Lanham, MD: Scarecrow, 2008).

12. Berkhof, *Systematic Theology*, 498.

13. J. I. Packer, "Faith," in *Evangelical Dictionary of Theology*, 3rd ed., ed. Daniel J. Treier and Walter A. Elwell (Grand Rapids: Baker Academic, 2017), 304.

14. For an alternative perspective, see Benjamin Myers, "Faith as Self-Understanding: Towards a Post-Barthian Appreciation of Rudolf Bultmann," *International Journal of Systematic Theology* 10, no. 1 (2008): 21–35.

15. Reinhold Niebuhr, "Faith as the Sense of Meaning in Human Existence," *Christianity and Crisis*, June 13, 1966, 121–29.

16. Mark A. Maddix and Richard P. Thompson, "Scripture as Formation: The Role of Scripture in Christian Formation," *Wesleyan Theological Journal* 46, no. 1 (2011): 134–49.

17. Mark A. Maddix and Richard P. Thompson, "Scripture as Formation: The Role of Scripture in Christian Formation," *Christian Education Journal*, 3rd series supplement, 9 (2012): S79–S93.

18. Christopher Ben Simpson, *Modern Christian Theology* (New York: Bloomsbury T&T Clark, 2016), 19.

19. Steven D. Cone, *Theology from the Great Tradition* (New York: Bloomsbury T&T Clark, 2018), 92 (emphasis added).

20. Dieter Lührmann, "Faith: New Testament," in *Anchor Bible Dictionary*, vol. 2, ed. David Noel Freedman (New York: Doubleday, 1992), 756.

21. Louis Berkhof, *The History of Christian Doctrine* (Grand Rapids: Eerdmans, 1937), 204.

22. Bromiley, *Historical Theology*, 39–40.

23. Augustine, *De doctrina Christiana* 40.60, cited in Alister E. McGrath, ed., *The Christian Theology Reader*, 3rd ed. (Malden, MA: Blackwell, 2007), 8.

24. Alister E. McGrath, *Historical Theology: An Introduction in the History of Christian Thought* (Oxford: Blackwell, 1999), 118–19.

25. E. H. Klotsche, *The History of Christian Doctrine*, rev. ed. (Grand Rapids: Baker, 1979), 145.

26. Cone, *Theology from the Great Tradition*, 92.

27. Calvin, *Institutes* 3.2.2.

28. Calvin, *Institutes* 3.2.6.

29. David C. Steinmetz, "Luther and Formation in Faith," in *Educating the People of Faith*, ed. John Van Engen (Grand Rapids: Eerdmans, 2004), 253–69.

30. John G. Stackhouse, *Evangelical Landscapes: Facing Critical Issues of the Day* (Grand Rapids: Baker Academic, 2002), 193.

31. Christopher Gehrz and Mark Pattie III, *The Pietist Option* (Wheaton: IVP Academic, 2017), 69.

32. Gehrz and Pattie, *Pietist Option*, 71.

33. For more on Pietism, see James Riley Estep Jr., "Scripture and Spiritual Formation in German Pietism," *Christian Education Journal* 9 (Spring 2012): S94–S109.

34. John L. Elias, *A History of Christian Education* (Malabar, FL: Krieger, 2020), 111–12.

35. F. Ernest Stoeffler, "Can These Bones Live?," *Church History* 5, no. 2 (n.d.): 9.

36. Philipp Jakob Spener, *Pia Desideria*, trans. and ed. Theodore G. Tappert (Philadelphia: Fortress, 1964), 46.

37. Peter C. Erb, ed., *Pietists: Selected Writings* (New York: Paulist Press, 1983), 58.

38. F. Ernest Stoeffler, *German Pietism during the Eighteenth Century*, Studies in the History of Religions 24 (Leiden: Brill, 1973), 22.

39. Erb, *Pietists*, 69–70.

40. Erb, *Pietists*, 69.

41. Erb, *Pietists*, 69.

42. Erb, *Pietists*, 70.

43. Stoeffler, "Can These Bones Live?," 16.

44. Spener, *Pia Desideria*, 103.

45. "Slacktivism," Urban Dictionary, accessed May 15, 2018, https://www.urbandictionary.com/define.php?term=slacktivism.

46. See the critique of such ideas in Jack Cottrell, *The Faith Once for All* (Joplin, MO: College Press, 2002), 326–27.

47. Cottrell, *The Faith Once for All*, 329–30.

48. Berkhof, *Systematic Theology*, 505.

49. Klotsche, *History of Christian Doctrine*, 145.

50. McGrath, *Christian Theology Reader*, 441–45.

51. Gehrz and Pattie, *Pietist Option*, 71.

52. See Richard B. Hughes, *The Faith of Jesus Christ*, 2nd ed. (Grand Rapids: Eerdmans, 2002).

53. Stephen D. Lowe and Mary E. Lowe, "Allēlōn: Reciprocal Commands and Christian Development," *Christian Education Journal*, 3rd series, 7, no. 2 (2010): 281.

54. Maddix and Thompson, "Scripture as Formation" (*Christian Education Journal*), S90–S91.

55. David Setran, "Igniting the 'Family Sacrifice': Cotton Mather and Familial Christian Education in Puritan New England," *Christian Education Journal*, 3rd series, 11, no. 2 (2014): 350–66.

Chapter 3: Faith Formation Theory Revised

1. James W. Fowler, *Stages of Faith: The Psychological Human Development and the Quest for Meaning* (San Francisco: Harper & Row, 1995).

2. Jean Piaget, *Genetic Epistemology* (New York: Columbia University Press, 1970).

3. Jonathan H. Kim, "Thema and Faith Formation," 2018 (unpublished raw data). This qualitative research was funded by the Lilly Endowment through the Association of Theological Schools grants program.

4. The use of the term *evangelical* in this chapter is limited to its biblical meaning. The word *evangelical* comes from the Greek word *euangelion* (εὐαγγέλιον), which means "gospel," "good news," or "message" of Jesus Christ. As a biblical concept, the term *evangelical* describes the salvific message regarding Christ's incarnation, suffering, death, and resurrection (Matt. 4:23; Acts 20:24; Rom. 16:25; Gal. 3:8; Eph. 1:13; Heb. 4:2, 6). Theologically speaking, *evangelical* typically refers to a person who believes in the person and work of Jesus Christ, who experienced the new life of regeneration, who lives the Spirit-directed life of obedience, and who affirms that the Bible is the ultimate authority on all issues of life and faith.

5. Since this chapter is not intended to be an exhaustive research report, the compilation and discussion of my research findings will be reserved for another venue. Thus, the focus is on describing the four stages of faith based on my study outcomes.

Chapter 4: A Critique of Faith Development Theory

1. Jeff Astley and Leslie Francis, eds., *Christian Perspectives on Faith Development: A Reader* (Grand Rapids: Eerdmans, 1992), vii.

2. Edward Piper, "Faith Development: A Critique of Fowler's Model and a Proposed Alternative," unpublished paper, accessed March 1, 2020, http://www.meadville.edu/files/resources/v3n1-piper-faith-development-a-critique-of-fowlers.pdf.

3. Timothy Paul Jones, "The Basis of James W. Fowler's Understanding of Faith in the Research of Wilfred Cantwell Smith: An Examination from an Evangelical Perspective," *Religious Education* 99, no. 4 (2004): 345–46.

4. C. Ellis Nelson, "Does Faith Develop? An Evaluation of Fowler's Position," in Astley and Francis, *Christian Perspectives on Faith Development*, 63–64.

5. James W. Fowler, *Stages of Faith: The Psychological Human Development and the Quest for Meaning* (San Francisco: Harper & Row, 1995), 3.

6. Fowler, *Stages of Faith*, 3–4.

7. Fowler, *Stages of Faith*, 17.

8. Perry Downs, *Teaching for Spiritual Growth* (Grand Rapids: Zondervan, 1995), 76; and Reinhold Niebuhr, *The Theology of Reinhold Niebuhr*, *The Review of Politics* (Notre Dame, IN: University of Notre Dame Press, 1961), 93–102.

9. Wilfred Cantwell Smith, *Faith and Belief: The Difference Between Them* (Princeton: Princeton University Press, 1998), 5–6.

10. Smith, *Faith and Belief*, 12.

11. Fowler, *Stages of Faith*, 14.

12. Fowler, *Stages of Faith*, 14.

13. James W. Fowler, "Faith Development at 30: Naming the Challenges of Faith in a New Millennium," *Religious Education* 99, no. 4 (2004): 412.

14. James W. Fowler, *Faithful Change: The Personal and Public Challenges of Postmodern Life* (Nashville: Abingdon, 1996), 57.

15. Jones, "Basis of James W. Fowler's Understanding of Faith," 349.

16. Astley and Francis, *Christian Perspectives on Faith Development*, xiii.

17. See James E. Loder and James W. Fowler, "Conversations on Fowler's *Stages of Faith* and Loder's *Transforming Moment*," *Religious Education* 77, no. 2 (1982): 133–48.

18. Marlene M. Jardine and Henning G. Viljeon, "Fowler's Theory of Faith Development: An Evaluative Discussion," *Religious Education* 88, no. 1 (1992): 75.

19. Astley and Francis, *Christian Perspectives on Faith Development*, xiv.

20. Jones, "Basis of James W. Fowler's Understanding of Faith," 354.

21. Loder and Fowler, "Conversations," 144.

22. Adapted from James E. Loder, *The Transforming Moment* (Colorado Springs: Helmers & Howard, 1989), 99–122. See also Dean G. Blevins and Mark A. Maddix, *Discovering Discipleship: Dynamics of Christian Education* (Kansas City, MO: Beacon Hill, 2010), 147.

23. James E. Loder, *The Transforming Moment* (Colorado Springs: Helmers & Howard, 1989), 128.

24. James W. Fowler, "Faith Development and the Postmodern Challenges," *International Journal for the Psychology of Religion* 11, no. 3 (2001): 160.

25. Romney J. Mischey, "Faith, Identity and Morality in Late Adolescence," in Astley and Francis, *Christian Perspectives on Faith Development*, 162.

26. Fowler, "Faith Development and the Postmodern Challenges," 160.

27. See Mark A. Maddix, "Unite the Pair So Long Disjoined: Justice and Empathy in Moral Development Theory," *Christian Education Journal* 8, no. 3 (2011): 46–63.

28. See Carol Gilligan, *In a Different Voice* (Cambridge: Harvard University Press, 1993); John C. Gibbs, *Moral Development and Reality: Beyond the Theories of Kohlberg and Hoffman* (Boston: Allyn and Bacon, 2009); and Maddix, "Unite the Pair So Long Disjoined."

29. Jardine and Viljeon, "Fowler's Theory of Faith Development," 76.

30. Maria Harris and Gabriel Moran, *Reshaping Religious Education: Conversations on Contemporary Practice* (Louisville: Westminster John Knox, 1998), 4.

31. Harris and Moran, *Reshaping Religious Education*, 4.

32. Association of Theological Schools, "Racial/Ethnic Students Represent Largest Growth Area for Theological Schools," 2012, https://www.ats.edu/uploads/resources/publications-pre sentations/documents/racial-ethnic-growth.pdf.

33. James W. Fowler, foreword to Astley and Francis, *Christian Perspectives on Faith Development*, xii.

34. Gilligan, *In a Different Voice*, 29.

35. Gilligan, *In a Different Voice*, 26.

36. Joan M. Elifson and Katharine R. Stone, "Integrating Social, Moral, and Cognitive Development Theory: Implications of James Fowler's Epistemology Paradigm for Basic Writers," *Journal of Basic Writing* 4, no. 2 (1985): 26.

37. See Jean Baker Miller, *Toward a New Psychology of Women* (Boston: Beacon Press, 1976).

38. See Mary Field Belenky, Blythe McVicker Clinchy, Nancy Rule Goldberger, and Jill Mattuck Tarule, *Women's Ways of Knowing: The Development of Self, Voice, and Mind*, 10th ann. ed. (New York: BasicBooks, 1997).

39. Piper, "Faith Development."

40. "QuickFacts," United States Census Bureau, accessed March 1, 2020, https://www.census .gov/quickfacts/fact/table/US/PST045218.

41. Vanessa Walker and John Snarey, *Race-ing Moral Formation: African American Perspectives on Care and Justice* (New York: Teachers College Press, 2004), 4–5.

42. Rosalie A. Cohen, "Conceptual Styles, Culture Conflict and Nonverbal Tests of Intelligence," *American Anthropologist* 71 (1969): 828–29.

43. Elifson and Stone, "Integrating Social, Moral, and Cognitive," 25–26.

Chapter 5: Cultural Challenges to Faith Formation

1. Richard Niebuhr, *Christ and Culture* (New York: Harper & Row, 1951).

2. D. A. Carson, *Christ and Culture Revisited* (Grand Rapids: Eerdmans, 2008).

3. Carson, *Christ and Culture Revisited*, 171.

4. Carson, *Christ and Culture Revisited*, 172.

5. Andrew Root, *Faith Formation in a Secular Age* (Grand Rapids: Baker Academic, 2017), 103–12.

6. Stephen Prothero, *Religious Literacy* (New York: Harper & Collins, 2008).

7. Based in part on previously published articles: "Form without Substance," *Christian Standard*, November 30, 2008, 4–5, 8; "Deep Impact: The Cultural Challenge of Biblical Illiteracy," *Christian Standard*, February 2014, 12–15; and "What's Next in Biblical Literacy?," in *What's Next? How Thinking Forward Moves the Church Forward* (Indianapolis: e2 ministries, 2014), 121–32.

8. George Gallup Jr. and Jim Castelli, "Americans and the Bible," *Bible Review* 6, no. 3 (June 1990), https://www.baslibrary.org/bible-review/6/3/18.

9. David Van Biema, "The Case for Teaching the Bible," *Time*, April 2, 2007, 43.

10. Stephen Prothero, *Religious Literacy* (New York: Harper Collins, 2007), 30.

11. "Five Myths about Young Adult Church Dropouts," Barna Group, November 15, 2011, https://www.barna.com/research/five-myths-about-young-adult-church-dropouts.

12. Jason Daye, "Glenn Paauw: Pulling Back Bible Tradition in the Modern Era to Uncover God's Intention for the Scriptures," Church Leaders, April 5, 2017, http://churchleaders.com/pod cast/301817-glenn-paauw-pulling-back-bible-tradition-modern-era-uncover-gods-intention -scriptures.html.

13. Jason Daye, "Bible Literacy Experts Address the Problem of Bible-Less Christianity," Church Leaders, March 31, 2017, http://churchleaders.com/podcast/301605-bible-literacy-experts -address-problem-bible-less-christianity.html.

14. Jason Norris, "Biblical Illiteracy: Sounding the Alarm," Medium, April 23, 2015, https:// medium.com/@jasonenorris/biblical-illiteracy-in-the-church-6b85ac4864b9.

15. Marie Wachlin et al., *Bible Literacy Report* (Front Royal, VA: Biblical Literacy Project, 2005), 6.

16. Wachlin et al., *Bible Literacy Report*, 25.

17. Collin Hansen, "Why Johnny Can't Read the Bible," *Christianity Today*, May 2010, 38.

18. Brad J. Waggoner, *The Shape of Faith to Come: Spiritual Formation and the Future of Discipleship* (Nashville: B&H, 2008), 70.

19. Daye, "Bible Literacy Experts."

20. Glenn R. Paauw, *Saving the Bible from Ourselves* (Downers Grove, IL: InterVarsity, 2016), 11–12.

21. Andrew Root, "Faith Formation in a Secular Age," *Word and World* 37, no. 2 (2017): 131–32.

22. Christian Smith with Melinda Lundquist Denton, *Soul Searching: The Religious and Spiritual Lives of American Teenagers* (New York: Oxford University Press, 2005), 162–70.

23. Smith with Denton, *Soul Searching*, 162–63; cf. also Kenda Creasy Dean, *Almost Christian* (New York: Oxford University Press, 2010), 14.

24. Christian Smith with Patricia Snell, *Souls in Transition* (New York: Oxford University Press, 2009), 154–55.

25. Smith with Snell, *Souls in Transition*, 155.

26. Smith with Snell, *Souls in Transition*, 156–63.

27. Dean, *Almost Christian*, 39.

28. Root, "Faith Formation in a Secular Age," 155.

29. Dean, *Almost Christian*, 29–30.

30. Nels F. S. Ferré, *Christian Faith and Higher Education* (New York: Harper & Brothers, 1954), 80.

31. Lawrence O. Richards, "Critical Thinking and Christian Perspective," *Christian Education Journal* 15, no. 1 (1994): 17–19.

32. Jack Dean Kingsbury, *Conflict in Mark: Jesus, Authorities, Disciples* (Minneapolis: Augsburg Fortress, 1991), 85–89.

33. Richards, "Critical Thinking and Christian Perspective," 15.

34. George W. Stickel, "The Definition of Critical Thought and Its Implications for Christian Education," *Christian Education Journal* 15, no. 1 (1994): 33–41.

35. Michael Warren, "The Sacramentality of Critique and Its Challenge for Christian Educators," *Christian Education Journal* 15, no. 1 (1994): 49.

36. Eugene C. Roehlkepartain and Eboo Patel, "Congregations: Unexamined Crucibles for Spiritual Development," in *The Handbook of Spiritual Development in Childhood and Adolescence*, ed. Eugene C. Roehlkepartain, Pamela Ebstyne King, Linda Wagener, and Peter L. Benson (Thousand Oaks, CA: Sage, 2009), 61–62.

37. Based on a presentation at the Baptist Association of Christian Educators, New Orleans Baptist Theological Seminary (2017), later published as Randy Stone, John McClendon, and Jim Estep, *Indispensable: Becoming a MVP in Disciple-Making* (self-pub., CreateSpace, 2018).

38. Glenn M. Vernon, "Religious 'Nones': A Neglected Category," *Journal for the Scientific Study of Religion* 7, no. 2 (1968): 219.

39. Robert Putnam and David Campbell, "The Young 'Nones,'" *Christian Century*, November 30, 2010, 7.

40. John G. Condran and Joseph B. Tamney, "Religious 'Nones': 1957 to 1982," *Sociological Analysis* 46, no. 4 (1985): 415–23.

41. Condran and Tamney, "Religious 'Nones,'" 419.

42. Chaeyoon Lim, Carol Ann MacGregor, and Robert D. Putnam, "Secular and Liminal: Discovering Heterogeneity among Religious Nones," *Journal for the Scientific Study of Religion* 49, no. 4 (2010): 596–618.

43. Joseph O'Brian Baker and Buster Smith, "None Too Simple: Examining Issues of Religious Nonbelief and Nonbelonging in the United States," *Journal for the Scientific Study of Religion* 48, no. 4 (2009): 719–33.

44. Lim, MacGregor, and Putnam, "Secular and Liminal," 613.

45. Elizabeth Drescher, *Choosing Our Religion: The Spiritual Lives of America's Nones* (New York: Oxford University Press, 2016), loc. 358, 3720 of 5616, Kindle; and Lim, MacGregor, and Putnam, "Secular and Liminal," 613–14.

46. Lim, MacGregor, and Putnam, "Secular and Liminal," 613–14.

47. Kaya Oakes, *The Nones Are Alright: A New Generation of Believers, Seekers and Those in Between* (Maryknoll, NY: Orbis, 2015), loc. 246 of 3314, Kindle.

48. Lim, MacGregor, and Putnam, "Secular and Liminal," 396.

49. Lim, MacGregor, and Putnam, "Secular and Liminal," 614.

50. Drew Dyck, "How Can Churches Reach Nominal Believers before They Become 'Nones'?," *Christianity Today*, March 2014, 24.

51. Joseph B. Tamney, Shawn Powell, and Stephen Johnson, "Innovation Theory and Religious Nones," *Journal for the Scientific Study of Religion* 28, no. 2 (1989): 223.

52. Baker and Smith, "None Too Simple," 732; Drescher, *Choosing Our Religion*, loc. 5564 of 5616, Kindle; and Jonathan P. Hill, *Emerging Adulthood and Faith* (Grand Rapids: Calvin University Press, 2015), loc. 260 of 919, Kindle.

53. Alec Baldwin, "One thing that is changed forever in this country is the meaning of the word 'Christian' as it applies to politics," Twitter, November 9, 2016, 12:39 a.m., https://twitter.com/ABFalecbaldwin/status/796225586549129217.

54. Drescher, *Choosing Our Religion*, loc. 2645 of 5616, Kindle.

55. Cf. Baker and Smith, "None Too Simple," 732.

56. Teri McDowell Ott, "In the Realm of the Nones," *Christian Century*, January 6, 2016, 28.

57. Lim, MacGregor, and Putnam, "Secular and Liminal," 615.

58. James Emery White, *The Rise of the Nones* (Grand Rapids: Baker Books, 2014), 31–42.

59. Caryn D. Riswold, "Teaching the College 'Nones': Christian Privilege and the Religion Professor," *Teaching Theology and Religion* 18, no. 2 (2015): 133–48.

60. Cf. Oakes, *The Nones Are Alright,* loc. 3301 of 3314, Kindle.

61. Drescher, *Choosing Our Religion,* loc. 422 of 5616, Kindle; Ott, "In the Realm of the Nones," 28.

62. C. Kirk Hadaway and Wade Clark Roof, "Those Who Stay Religious 'Nones' and Those Who Don't: A Research Note," *Journal for the Scientific Study of Religion* 18, no. 2 (1979): 199.

63. Oakes, *The Nones Are Alright,* loc. 642 of 3314, Kindle.

64. Ott, "In the Realm of the Nones," 28.

65. Oakes, *The Nones Are Alright,* loc. 2653 of 3314, Kindle.

66. Riswold, "Teaching the College 'Nones,'" 140–45.

67. Dyck, "How Can Churches," 24.

68. Dyck, "How Can Churches," 24.

Chapter 6: Faith Formation in Community

1. John Wesley, "Preface to *Hymns and Sacred Poems* (1739)," in *Doctrinal and Controversial Treatises II,* ed. Paul Wesley Chilcote and Kenneth J. Collins, vol. 13 of *The Works of John Wesley* (Nashville: Abingdon, 2013), 39.

2. Horace Bushnell, *Christian Nurture* (New York: Charles Scribner, 1861), 10.

3. Perry Downs, "Christian Nurture: A Comparison of Horace Bushnell and Lawrence O. Richards," *Christian Education Journal* 4, no. 2 (1983): 44.

4. Robert B. Mullin, *The Puritan as Yankee: The Life of Horace Bushnell* (Grand Rapids: Eerdmans, 2002), 118.

5. Downs, "Christian Nurture," 45.

6. Bushnell, *Christian Nurture,* 76.

7. Downs, "Christian Nurture," 45.

8. Bushnell, *Christian Nurture,* 26–27.

9. George Albert Coe, *A Social Theory of Religious Education* (New York: Scribner's Sons, 1929), 181.

10. Howard Burgess, *Models of Religious Education* (Wheaton: Victor Books, 1996), 81–82.

11. C. Ellis Nelson, "Socialization Revisited," *Union Seminary Review* 47, nos. 3–4 (1993): 162.

12. Nelson, "Socialization Revisited," 52.

13. Burgess, *Models of Religious Education,* 117.

14. Perry Downs, *Teaching for Spiritual Growth* (Grand Rapids: Zondervan, 1994), 159.

15. John Westerhoff and O. C. Edwards Jr., eds., *A Faithful Church: Issues in the History of Catechesis* (Wilton, CT: Morehouse-Barlow, 1981).

16. John Westerhoff, "A Discipline in Crisis," *Religious Education* 74, no. 1 (1979): 7–15.

17. John Westerhoff, *Learning through Liturgy* (New York: Seabury, 1978).

18. John Westerhoff, "Formation, Education, Instruction," *Religious Education* 52, no. 4 (1987): 582.

19. Westerhoff, "Discipline in Crisis," 13.

20. John Westerhoff, "The Shaking of the Foundation," in *A Reader in Christian Education,* ed. E. Gibbs (Grand Rapids: Baker, 1992), 241.

21. John Westerhoff, *Values for Tomorrow's Children: An Alternative Future for Education in the Church* (Philadelphia: Pilgrim's Press, 1970).

22. John Westerhoff, *Living the Faith Community: The Church That Makes a Difference* (Minneapolis: Winston Press, 1985), 23.

23. Westerhoff, *Living the Faith Community,* 25.

24. Westerhoff, *Living the Faith Community*, 85.
25. Phillip W. Sell, "Lawrence O. Richards," Biola University, accessed March 1, 2020, https://www.biola.edu/talbot/ce20/database/lawrence-o-richards.
26. Charles Foster, *Educating Congregations: The Future of Christian Education* (Nashville: Abingdon, 1994), 13.
27. Jack L. Seymour, ed., *Mapping Christian Education: Approaches to Congregational Learning* (Nashville: Abingdon, 1997), 21.
28. Foster, *Educating Congregations*, 23–24.
29. Sondra Higgins Matthaei, *Formation in Faith: The Congregational Ministry of Making Disciples* (Nashville: Abingdon, 2008), 13–14.
30. Robert W. Pazmiño, *Foundational Issues in Christian Education* (Grand Rapids: Baker, 1997), 45.
31. Ruth C. Duck, *Worship for the Whole People of God: Vital Worship for the 21st Century* (Louisville: Westminster John Knox, 2013), 3.
32. Brent Peterson, *Created to Worship: God's Invitation to Become Fully Human* (Kansas City, MO: Beacon Hill, 2012), 54–55.
33. Debra Dean Murphy, *Teaching That Transforms: Worship as the Heart of Christian Education* (Grand Rapids: Brazos, 2004), 10.
34. Westerhoff, *Living the Faith Community*, 23.
35. Westerhoff, *Living the Faith Community*, 85.
36. Foster, *Educating Congregations*, 45.
37. Foster, *Educating Congregations*, 46.
38. See Mark Maddix and Jay Akkerman, eds., *Missional Discipleship: Partners in God's Redemptive Mission in the World* (Kansas City, MO: Beacon Hill, 2013).

Chapter 7: The Role of Scripture in Faith Formation

1. George Lyons, "Knowing the Scriptures: How to Study the Bible as Spiritual Formation," in *Spiritual Formation: A Wesleyan Paradigm*, ed. Diane Leclerc and Mark A. Maddix (Kansas City, MO: Beacon Hill, 2011), 19.
2. Bob Smietana, "LifeWay Research: Americans Are Fond of the Bible, Don't Actually Read It," LifeWay Research, April 25, 2017, https://lifewayresearch.com/2017/04/25/lifeway-research-americans-are-fond-of-the-bible-dont-actually-read-it.
3. "Frequency of Reading Scripture," Pew Research Center, accessed March 1, 2020, https://www.pewforum.org/religious-landscape-study/frequency-of-reading-scripture.
4. See Michael Lodahl, *The Story of God: A Narrative Theology* (Kansas City, MO: Beacon Hill, 2008).
5. See William J. Abraham, *Canon and Criterion in Christian Theology* (Oxford: Oxford University Press, 1998), 1–56.
6. Mark A. Maddix and Richard P. Thompson, "Scripture as Formation: The Role of Scripture in Christian Formation," *Wesleyan Theological Journal* 46, no. 1 (Spring 2011): 136.
7. Maddix and Thompson, "Scripture as Formation," 137–40.
8. See Richard P. Thompson, "Inspired Imagination: John Wesley's Concept of Biblical Inspiration and Literary-Critical Studies," in *Reading the Bible in Wesleyan Ways: Some Constructive Proposals*, ed. Barry L. Callen and Richard P. Thompson (Kansas City, MO: Beacon Hill, 2004), 66–73.
9. Barbara E. Bowe, *Biblical Foundations of Spirituality: Touching a Finger to the Flame* (Lanham, MD: Sheed and Ward, 2003), 13.
10. Sandra M. Schneiders, "Biblical Spirituality," *Interpretation* 56, no. 2 (2002): 136.
11. See Eugene H. Peterson, "Eat This Book: The Holy Community at Table with the Holy Scripture," *Theology Today* 56, no. 1 (1999): 5–17.
12. Bowe, *Biblical Foundations of Spirituality*, 177–78.

13. M. Robert Mullholland, *Shaped by the Word: The Power of Scripture in Spiritual Formation* (Nashville: Upper Room, 1985), 55–60.

14. John Wesley, *The Works of John Wesley*, 3rd ed., ed. Thomas Jackson (London: Wesleyan Methodist Book Room, 1872), 14:243; Mullholland, *Shaped by the Word*, 147–48.

15. John Wesley, *Expository Notes on the Old Testament* (Salem, OH: Schmul, 1975), 9.

16. Schneiders, "Biblical Spirituality," 133–42.

17. Preaching is explored in greater detail in chapter 6.

18. Worship is explored in greater detail in chapter 6.

19. Schneiders, "Biblical Spirituality," 138.

20. Mark A. Maddix and James R. Estep Jr., *Practicing Christian Education: An Introduction to Ministry* (Grand Rapids: Baker Academic, 2017), 65.

21. See D. Burton-Christie, *The Word in the Desert: Scripture and the Quest for Holiness in Early Church Monasticism* (New York: Oxford University Press, 1993).

22. Marjorie Thompson, *Soul Feast: An Invitation to the Christian Spiritual Life* (Louisville: Westminster John Knox, 2014), 22.

23. Richard Peace, *Contemplative Bible Reading: Experiencing God through Scripture* (Eugene, OR: Wipf & Stock, 2015), 18.

Chapter 8: Forming Faith through Missions

1. William Dyrness, "Mercy Triumphs over Justice: James 2:13 and the Theology of Faith and Works," *Themelios* 6, no. 3 (April 1981): 11–16.

2. Jim Putman, "Here Are 6 Things Jesus Did to Equip His Disciples for Ministry," Jim Putman.com, July 8, 2018, http://jimputman.com/2018/07/08/6-things-jesus-did-to-equip-his -disciples-for-ministry.

3. Stephen Fortosis and Ken Garland, "Adolescent Cognitive Development," *Religious Education* 85, no. 4 (1990): 642.

4. Stephen Fortosis, "Theological Foundations for a Stage Model of Spiritual Formation," *Christian Education Journal* 96, no. 1 (2001): 49–63.

5. Michael S. Wilder and Shane W. Parker, *Transformission: Making Disciples through Short-Term Missions* (Nashville: B&H, 2010).

6. Wilder and Parker, *Transformission*, 140.

7. Terence D. Linhart, "Planting Seeds: The Curricular Hope of Short-Term Mission Experiences in Youth Ministry," *Christian Education Journal* 3, no. 2 (2005): 261–62.

8. Fortosis and Garland, "Adolescent Cognitive Development," 640–44.

9. P. L. Benson and C. H. Eklin, *Effective Christian Education: A National Study of Protestant Congregations* (Minneapolis: Search Institute, 1990).

10. Stephen T. Beers, "The Effects of a Study Abroad/Mission Trip on the Faith Development of College Students," *Growth* 1, no. 1 (2014): 100.

11. Beers, "Effects of a Study Abroad," 100.

12. Terence D. Linhart, "'They Were So Alive!': The Spectacle Self and Youth Group Short-Term Mission Trips," *Missiology* 34, no. 4 (2006): 453–56.

13. Jim Henderson and Matt Casper, *Jim and Casper Go to Church* (Carol Stream, IL: Tyndale, 2007).

14. Linhart, "Planting Seeds," 263.

15. Kurt Alan Ver Beek, "The Impact on Short-Term Missions: A Case Study of House Construction in Honduras after Hurricane," *Missiology* 34, no. 4 (2006): 485.

16. Conrad Swartzentruber, "The Impact of a Mission Trip: Preparing Students to Change Our World," *Christian School Education* 12, no. 2 (2008–9), https://www.acsi.org/resources /cse/cse-magazine/the-impact-of-a-mission-trip-preparing-students-to-change-our-world-122.

17. Swartzentruber, "Impact of a Mission Trip."

18. Swartzentruber, "Impact of a Mission Trip."

19. Linhart, "'They Were So Alive!'," 452–53.
20. Linhart, "Planting Seeds," 265. See also Wilder and Parker, *Transformission*, 143.
21. Cf. Kenneth Botton, Chuck King, and Junius Venugopal, "Education for Spirituality," *Christian Education Journal* 1NS (1997): 44–47.

Chapter 9: Faith Formation in Multiethnic Contexts

1. James W. Fowler, *Stages of Faith: The Psychological Human Development and the Quest for Meaning* (San Francisco: Harper & Row, 1995); Janet O. Hagberg and Robert A. Guelich, *The Critical Journey: Stages in the Life of Faith* (Salem, WI: Sheffield, 2004); M. Scott Peck, *The Road Less Travelled: The Unending Journey toward Spiritual Growth* (New York: Simon & Schuster, 1978); Larry Stephens, *Building for Your Child's Faith* (Grand Rapids: Zondervan, 1996); John H. Westerhoff, *Will Our Children Have Faith?* (New York: Seabury, 1976); Mary Wilcox, *Developmental Journey* (Nashville: Abingdon, 1979).
2. Paul Hiebert, *Cultural Anthropology* (Grand Rapids: Baker, 1983), 25.
3. "QuickFacts," United States Census Bureau, accessed March 1, 2020, https://www.census.gov/quickfacts/fact/table/US/PST045216; Hamilton Lombard, "Will Whites Be a Minority by 2040?," Stat Chat, July 25, 2017, http://statchatva.org/2017/07/25/will-whites-actually-be-a-minority-by-2040.
4. R. Stark, *The Rise of Christianity: A Sociologist Reconsiders History* (Princeton: Princeton University Press, 1996), 27, 158.
5. Diane M. Mackie, Eliot R. Smith, and Devin G. Ray, "Intergroup Emotions and Intergroup Relations," *Social and Personal Psychology Compass* 2, no. 5 (2008): 1866–80.

Chapter 10: Faith Formation in Global Contexts

1. Todd M. Johnson, *Christianity in Its Global Context, 1970–2020: Society, Religion, and Mission* (South Hamilton, MA: Gordon-Conwell Theological Seminary Center for the Study of Global Christianity, 2013), 13.
2. Johnson, *Christianity in Its Global Context*, 14.
3. Johnson, *Christianity in Its Global Context*, 22–33, 34–43, 54–61.
4. Johnson, *Christianity in Its Global Context*, 82.
5. The term *third culture* was first coined by an American anthropologist, Ruth Hill Useem, based on her study of overseas Americans in India (1952–53 and 1958). Though the formulation of the third-culture worldview is based on the fusion of multiple cultures, it contains a new perspective that is neither the home nor the host culture. It is composed of a very distinct cultural mixture and exists under the dialectic tension of negotiation and reinvention.

Index